BLOOD AND HONOR

Kerstan

Special Crusade Edition printed for
the Billy Graham Evangelistic Association

W⊕rld Wide

A ministry of the Billy Graham Association

1303 Hennepin Avenue
Minneapolis, Minnesota 55403

This edition is published with permission from the original publisher, David C. Cook Publishing Company, 850 North Grove, Elgin, Illinois 60120.

COVER DESIGN AND ILLUSTRATION BY BILL WORCESTER

ISBN 0-89191-192-8

LC 79-57520

Foreword

One of the most unforgettable events of my entire ministry was the opportunity in 1982 to preach the gospel of Jesus Christ throughout East Germany. Night after night, we saw hundreds of people make their commitment to Jesus Christ. By far the largest number were young people, vowing to follow Christ as their Savior and Lord wherever he might lead.

My interpreter in East Germany was Dr. Reinhold Kerstan, who tells in this book the remarkable story of his years as a member of the German Hitler Youth during World War II. As he and I traveled together, we could not help but think of that earlier generation of German young people, a generation that had vowed to follow not Christ, but another leader—Adolf Hitler—wherever he might lead them. Reinhold Kerstan knew that generation well, for he had been one of them. And yet by God's grace, he not only survived the horrors of the second World War but found in Jesus Christ the true meaning and hope of life.

This is a profoundly moving and inspiring story. It vividly portrays the false promises and deceptions of Nazism, and the despair and struggle for survival that characterized the months immediately after the war. But it also is a true story of forgiveness and healing, of compassion and new life. Most of all, it is a powerful testimony to the faithfulness and grace of God.

May God use this book to show each of us the importance of living for Christ each day—in our families, our jobs, our communities and nation, our world. And may God use it also to teach us more about his love and care for each of us in every circumstance.

BILLY GRAHAM

WITTENBERG, EAST GERMANY

Billy Graham and his interpreter, Reinhold Kerstan, preaching to 1,500 at historic Wittenberg, birthplace of the Reformation, from the same pulpit that Martin Luther used for many years.

Reinhold Kerstan interprets for Billy Graham, who is preaching from pulpit of Trinity Church in Gorlitz, East Germany, on the Polish border.

MAGDEBURG, E. GERMANY
Billy Graham visits a Christian Book Store in Magdeburg, E. Germany, during his six-city preaching tour of the German Democratic Republic.

Laying a wreath at Sachsenhausen, East Germany, concentration camp.

Dedicated to my children,
Andrew, Peter and Annette,
whose young lives have been
so much more peaceful than mine,
and whose concepts of "blood and honor"
were not twisted by Nazi ideology.
May God guide them safely
through the turmoil of their time.

Prologue

Holocaust, although it was fiction, was a dramatic and realistic portrayal of events during World War II. Having lived in Germany as a boy, I knew much of the story first-hand, and I intended to watch the series for four nights on television.

By the end of Part I on the first night, however, I was deeply troubled. What I had expected to be an evening of entertainment had become a traumatic, soulwrenching experience. On the second night I knew I couldn't sit there in the livingroom with my family and watch. They knew nothing of the horrors of the war. My wife, Inger, born and raised in Sweden, was proud that her country had kept its political neutrality for almost two-hundred years. Our three children, born in Switzerland, Canada, and the United States, had learned about Adolf Hitler and those sad pages of German history in school. We lived in a comfortable Chicago suburb more than thirty years later, and it meant very little to them.

So, on the second night, I slipped out of the living-room and went downstairs to the den to watch on a small black and white set. . . I needed to be alone.

A few minutes later, however, our oldest son, Andrew, came down.

"Aren't you going to watch 'Holocaust,' Dad?"

"Yes, Andrew."

"But why are you sitting here by yourself?"

I hesitated, biting my lip, then I mumbled, "It's all right, son."

He must have sensed the uproar inside me, because he came back in a few minutes, placed a throw pillow on the floor beside me and started watching.

Or was he watching me, I wondered. How did he cope with the fact that his father was a product of the nation that had deliberately destroyed six million Jewish men, women, and children? Did it trouble him to know that I had, as a boy, clicked my heels, raised my stiff right arm, and cried, "Heil Hitler"?

Soon we were both totally absorbed in the events on the screen. Most of the action took place in Berlin where I had lived for sixteen years. Dr. Josef Weiss was a fictional character, but our family doctor had also been a Jew. And just as Berta Weiss, Josef's wife, was an accomplished musician, so our doctor's wife, Mrs. Gruenbaum, had been a talented pianist. Their piano, which we had bought for a token, enhanced our home through most of the war.

On that second night of the film, I saw the Weiss family struggle to cope with conditions in the Warsaw Ghetto and in Buchenwald. And there were Erik and Marta Dorf, proud, ambitious young Germans, playing their infamous parts in the Third Reich. I had known families like the Dorfs. I had remembered some of them just a few years ago when I stood at Babi Yar, the deep ravine outside Kiev in the USSR, where Nazi SS commandos had massacred 33,000 Jews in two days.

For years, however, I had disclaimed any connection with the atrocities. After all, I had been just a kid of eight when the war broke out. And all through those dismal years, I had known nothing of a "holocaust." Yet the fact that I had grown up among the people who sought to exterminate European Jewry kept haunting me.

"Dad, I love you!" Andrew had moved closer to me, his shoulder touching mine.

Oh, no, this husky eighteen-year-old shouldn't have said that. Now I couldn't hold back the tears.

"You feel low, don't you?"

I could only nod and wipe my eyes.

George Santayana has warned us that "those who do not remember the past are condemned to relive it." I wanted to remember. Yes, I wanted to remember so that I would not have to relive those tragic years and so that neither my children nor their children would ever have to know anything like it. I wanted to know that it would not, could not, ever happen again.

How had it all begun? What had shaped my mind and my life to make me, a believer in Christ at that young age, also a believer in a master race? What had led to the broken dream and to my frantic flight as a refugee across a war-torn continent?

It wasn't any one incident, of course, but a series of subtle influences and events that swept me along. Actually I hadn't known many Jews. I was an "Aryan," but I was also a Christian. My father was the pastor of a church, and he and my mother had taught me well. But my faith in God and my love for the Bible bothered my friends and teachers. In their view there was no room for fairy tales and a weak reliance on some external force—at least not for a German boy.

The real struggle came when my school was evacuated from Berlin to the relative safety of Czechoslovakia. There the pervasive religion of the state, as well as plain human cruelty, began to squeeze out the Christianity I had seen and lived at home. I tried to keep my faith alive against the pressures, the taunts, and the persecution of both teachers and classmates. But day by day I found myself slipping, being pulled back further and further into a godless, Hitler-centered world.

At the same time I received letters of encouragement from my parents, quoting the Scriptures, reminding me of the truths they taught me. And I knew that though my father was fighting on some faraway front, and my mother was holding out alone in Berlin, their prayers were building a wall of protection around me.

In one sense my story is an exposé of an ideology at work. It's a cutaway version of the system—Nazism—as it worked in the mind of one child, trying to capture him and make him in its image. And in the telling we understand more clearly what could happen at some other time, in some other place, with some other "ism."

But my story is also a living example of the promise of Proverbs 22:6—"Train up a child in the way he should go, and when he is old he will not depart from it." My parents had taught me to pray. From them I had learned to love and enjoy reading the Bible. They showed me that Jesus Christ was more than a faraway figure from New Testament times. He was real, a person, God, someone who spoke to me through his Word.

I survived physically, not because I was tougher or better than those around me, but because, by the grace of God, he wanted me to. I survived spiritually, not because I was more pious or more religious than my peers, but because my parents had implanted deeply in me, at an early age, a love for God and his Son, Jesus Christ. They had trained me in the godly way they wanted me to go, and as I grew I did not depart from it.

I

I treasured every minute of the train ride to Prague. I hadn't seen my father very much in the last few years of the war, and now he was taking me to the relative safety of Czechoslovakia where my school, the Lettow-Vorbeck-Oberschule, had been evacuated. He sat stiff and proud in his army uniform with the *Hauptfeldwebel* (sergeant major) insignia and an armband for the "Propaganda Kompanie." It was August 1944.

I had a uniform, too—brown shirt, black pants and jacket, and on my shirtsleeve an emblem of lightning, symbolizing victory. I was a member of the Hitler Youth, and I sat erect beside my father as the train crossed the sun-baked fields of Bavaria.*

The farewell scene with my mother lingered in my mind. "God bless you, my son," she had said, putting

*For a map of the locations mentioned in this book, see pages 174 and 175.

her hand on my head in a gesture of blessing. Then the tears had run, and she had hugged me tightly, as though to keep me from leaving.

But I had not wept. I had heard over and over again that a German boy does not weep. I wanted to cry. I was excited about going off to school and happy to be with my father, yet I wanted to cling to my mother and tell her how much I'd miss her. Instead I pushed those feelings down and assured her that I'd write often. Then, without looking back, I walked away.

Suddenly the train entered a tunnel, plunging us into darkness, and I reached quickly for my father's hand. I wondered as I did so if it was a sign of weakness, but in the darkness my hand touched my own military dagger at my side. "Blood and Honor" was engraved on the blade, and I would use it if I had to. We had entered Czechoslovakia, and the Czechs were Germany's enemies. They wouldn't hesitate to kill a German, and my hand tightened on the weapon.

As we broke into the light, however, I noticed my father sitting confidently, seemingly not afraid. He occasionally smiled at the Czech passengers, but I saw only hate in their grim stares. My father was a big man, almost bald, friendly, quick to smile. He had a shepherd-like appearance, and, indeed, he was the pastor of a church—at least before the war began.

We were the only two Germans in the compartment, and I marveled that he could sit there so unconcerned. In my young mind there was no question what the Czechs would do to us if they had a chance.

As the train neared the station, the passengers began to retrieve their luggage from the racks overhead, and a man leaned toward me.

"Prague is a beautiful city." He spoke in good German, and I realized that he must have understood everything I had said to my father about this country. Some of it wasn't too good.

The man continued, "People call it the Golden City. I hope you will see much beauty and gold there."

"Ja," another passenger picked up the conversation and scoffed. "There is still some gold in the streets, whatever you Germans haven't taken away."

The other passengers stared at the man who spoke so boldly to a German soldier, then hurriedly grabbed their bags and cases and were gone.

The first man was right. Prague is a showpiece of impressive bridges, Gothic cathedrals, castles, and it hadn't been bombed and burned as Berlin had. Czechoslovakia had been the second country on Adolf Hitler's list for expansion, after Austria. Actually he had little trouble taking the country. The defenseless Czechs had been sold out at the notorious Munich Conference, and France and England simply stood by while the Third Reich's finest marched in. That was five years ago, and now the Protectorate was overrun with German military.

We wandered through the broad streets together while we waited for the train to the suburbs. It gave me a child's delight when soldiers of lower rank than my father had to salute him first.

As a Hitler Youth I had learned to salute—although my first experience was not very pleasant. One day on the way to the market in Berlin, shortly after I had been inducted into the movement, I passed a German Youth leader without noticing. I didn't have my uniform on and wasn't watching for anyone, but suddenly I heard someone shout.

"Hey, Kerstan, halt."

I stopped, almost paralyzed, and a boy only a few years older than I stuck his face into mine. "Aren't you in my platoon?" I stood at attention, motionless and speechless.

"Is that how a German boy honors his leaders and the Fuehrer?" His voice grew louder and passersby began to watch. I could do nothing of course to defend myself, so it turned into a one-sided shouting match.

"I'll tell you what! Go back twenty-five yards, turn around and then salute me properly. On the double!"

Relieved, I dashed back the distance, made a stylish turn, and marched toward this preposterous platoon commander, who by now enjoyed the attention of the bystander. At the right moment I lifted my arm in salute and turned my head stiffly in his direction.

Then it was over.

Moments later in the market place, I had almost forgotten the scene, when a woman touched my shoulder.

"That leader of yours is crazy. Who does he think he is? Besides, you don't even have a uniform."

I knew she was right; yet something told me that she just didn't understand the New Order of which I had become a part and which I wanted to be my world. None of the older people would understand, our leaders had told us.

I had been born into Hitler Germany, however. I was not even two years old when Hitler was appointed chancellor. Germany had been in chaos as it entered the thirties. Exhausted by its defeat in World War I, then squeezed by depression, the nation was demoralized. Hitler and his band of National Socialists had held out the hope of restored pride, and the disillusioned people had thankfully grasped it. Once in power, he swiftly took control of every facet of German life to begin what he promised would be a thousand-year reign.

I had no idea how little time that Third Reich had left

to live. I was more interested that day in seeing my old classmates. From Prague we took the train a short distance to Rewnitz, then we walked the few blocks to the Villa Fragner, my new home.

"That's him, Father. That's Herr Grothe." I pointed out the headmaster as we walked through the iron gates and across a wide lawn.

The gray-haired teacher looked up from his garden work as we approached.

"Herr Grothe, I presume?" my father asked politely.

"Jawohl, correct. My name is Grothe," he replied quickly. His voice had a jarring sound that made me think of metal rubbing together.

"We are the Kerstans. This is my son Reinhold whom I leave in your care. Guten Tag!" Father had extended his hand to shake, but Mr. Grothe stepped back, raised his arm quickly and shouted, "Heil Hitler, Herr Hauptfeldwebel."

My father understood. In the new society there was no room for personal greeting, and especially for personal tokens of friendship during the war. All relationships were reduced to two words, "Heil Hitler!"

"You may come and look around, Herr Hauptfeldwebel, but there is really no need for that. We have one hundred boys here," the headmaster said stiffly. So instead of touring the Villa my father made ready to leave.

I couldn't remember one previous occasion when I had not kissed my father farewell, but I knew I would not do it this time. Not in front of Herr Grothe. As he bent to hug me, he sensed my embarrassment. He gave me a pat on the shoulder like a military buddy, turned on his heel, and walked out through the gate.

Loneliness and fear began to rumble someplace inside me as I watched his broad back disappear. But I had no time to feel sorry for myself.

"Come along, Reinhold," Herr Grothe interrupted my senseless staring.

"Ja, I will come." I answered obediently.

"What did you say?" he bellowed at me, and I looked up startled.

"You will always say, 'Jawohl,' here. Do you understand?"

"Ja, Herr. . . I mean, Jawohl."

Dejected and ashamed I followed him across the lawn and into the house, but I had lost all enthusiasm for exploring it. It was a large stucco house, appropriated, I learned, from a Jewish family. Mr. Grothe showed me a room with six bunks and explained that the boys from this room were gone for several weeks to help harvest the hop.

It was a stark room with the beds, twelve old wooden wardrobes, a large table, and twelve wooden chairs. Two small windows yielded some dim light, revealing the fact that there were no pictures on the walls, not even wallpaper. Mr. Grothe left me to put away my belongings, and I sat on a lower bunk and studied the bare walls.

Our apartment in Berlin was colorful. It radiated life and cheer and warmth, and I wondered when I'd ever see it again. As I arranged my belongings, Mr. Grothe came back into the room. He walked over to the shelf where I had arranged a few books and picked up my Bible.

"Well, what have we here?"

Mr. Grothe thumbed through the pages, then threw it in disgust on the bed. "You won't need that here, and you'll need the space for your school books."

The Bible was a familiar book to me. I had had one with pictures long before I could read, and I had read this one almost all the way through. The great men and women from the Old and New Testaments were my heroes. We read from it daily in our house, and my father had a collection of many translations and versions.

Naively I answered, "But I promised my parents I'd read it every day."

He studied me for a brief moment, then smiled condescendingly. "Your father is gone, and your mother isn't here." Then his voice grew sharper, "The Fuehrer has provided this place for you, and now you owe all your obedience to him. Frankly, I can't imagine that he'd want you to have that book on your shelf."

With a sick feeling I drew myself up and answered weakly, "Jawohl, Herr Grothe."

II

No one could have persuaded me during the summer of '44 that Germany would lose the war. It was obvious to the rest of the world, of course. Rome had fallen and the Allies had landed in Normandy in June. By late August they had entered Paris. On the eastern front the Russians had marched halfway across Poland.

We knew, however, that the war would turn around any minute, and I hoped that it would last at least a few more years so I would have a chance to fight. More and more Hitler Youth had been pressed into service on the front, and it seemed to be getting close to my turn.

School did not begin for several weeks and while we waited for the other boys to return, Mr. Grothe kept the skeleton crew busy raking, cutting wood, repairing whatever he could find that was broken. Most of our school was housed in the large hotel near the railroad station. For our meals, we had to march three times a day to the *Volkshaus,* about two kilometers away, to the tune of Mr. Grothe's strident commands.

As I listened to the Czech people around me, I discovered, strangely, that I could understand them. Their language sounded much like the Slavic language I had heard early in my life. The old people in East Prussia spoke a form of Polish they called Masuric. It lacked the proper Polish grammar and had none of the finesse the people of Warsaw put into their language, but it had a very distinct Slavic vocabulary. As I cautiously tried a few phrases here and there, I found I could speak colloquial Czech. The results generally startled the populace, who certainly didn't expect a brown-shirted German youth to speak their language.

One morning Mrs. Bata, the cleaning woman, could stand it no longer. She had come into my room early and we were the only ones there, when she suddenly asked where I come from and how I knew Czech. She stood there in a grandmotherly way with her thick arms and hands crossed over the mop handle, and I melted under her friendliness. Soon I found myself telling her my story.

I was born in Schwentainen, a village in East Prussia, on November 12, 1931. My parents had both come from Olschoewken, not many miles from there, and my father was a Baptist pastor.

I was just about to tell her of my brother, Siegfried, three years older than I, when the door was flung open. Mrs. Bata's arms went into automatic motion with the mop.

"Oh, there you are, Reinhold," Mr. Grothe growled at me. Then he noticed the Bible on my bed.

"So you've done all the pious stuff first," he sneered, "and wasted precious minutes in the day."

I had no defense, but Mrs. Bata came to my rescue.

"I think Reinhold sick today. He no look good in face. Just look at poor boy's tongue."

Before I could speak, Mr. Grothe scowled at me and rumbled, "All right, then, stay in bed. But we have no one to bring you food; so if you feel better at noon, it will be for your own good."

He slammed out and I sank back, relieved. But Mrs. Bata had no intention of letting me rest. One of her sons had died at about my age and she took on a motherly role. That morning I told her about all twelve years of my life.

I had enjoyed life in the country. Our house, part of the church building, stood at the end of a town of about eighteen hundred people. My father's church duties took him into the neighboring towns and villages several days a week, leaving my mother to visit the sick, feed the chickens, and look after two small boys.

My mother was a pretty woman with dark wavy hair, very efficient and practical. The pastor's house was the target of drifters and villagers in need looking for a handout or a place to sleep, and my kind-hearted father was quick to believe their stories. My mother, however, had a sharper eye for sorting out the fakers. Nevertheless, I remember many guests who suddenly appeared at the supper table or slept the night on the sofa in our living room, and Father, never sorry for being deceived, would happily quote, "It is more blessed to give than to receive."

We would often accompany my father as he visited his preaching stations. In a horse-drawn carriage we would ride through the thick East Prussian forests and prairies watching for wolves or foxes. My mother had a beautiful voice, and when she began singing the familiar hymns

23

we would all join her. When winter came, however, we'd heat big field stones to put in the bottom of the sled, then my brother and I would huddle under the heavy horsecarriage blankets hiding from the bitter cold and wind.

It seemed there was always a visitor, if not someone in need, then a relative, evangelist, or missionary. I liked the missionaries, and I would pump them for stories of adventure in exotic places. If their stories didn't match my imagination, I had no trouble adding the details from my own fertile mind.

Far from the capital of Berlin and in the innocence of my age, I had little inkling of the political turmoil and the clouds of war that were building. East Prussia had been separated from the rest of Germany by the Polish corridor. Germans resented the Treaty of Versailles that had created the division, and many of them recalled nostalgically the powerful and extensive German empire of years past. I had learned early in life the difference between Germans and Poles and the attending ethnic characteristics. Poles were Slavs—lazy, disorderly, inferior. We were Aryan, hard-working Germans.

When my uncles from America came to visit our isolated town, they brought a feeling of the new German identity that was growing worldwide. They were disappointed that only the school and the bürgermeister flew the German flag, so they built a flagpole in their parents' yard. Then each morning with pomp and ceremony they hoisted the swastika while another uncle took movies of the ritual.

When my father had to leave to do his military reserve duty, it didn't mean that much to me. He was home on the weekends, and I was proud of his clean, starched uniform. I imagined all kinds of war games that he played, but I took little notice of the dirt his uniform acquired during the week.

In the fall of 1937 my father received a call to serve a church in Berlin. I could hardly imagine that great city. I had seen pictures of its wide boulevards and linden trees, its concert halls and grand government buildings, its millions of people in tall apartment buildings.

The world was keeping a wary eye on Berlin in 1937. Hitler, the Fuehrer, had actually brought the country out of the depths of depression. With a combination of borrowed money and forced austerity, the Nazis had increased production, provided jobs, and rallied the national spirit. The red flag with its black swastika waved over every corner of the city, and brown-shirted troops marched stiff legged through the streets. In the chancellery, Hitler laid plans for the conquest of Europe and proclaimed that "the German form of life is determined for the next thousand years."

When time came for us to leave East Prussia, the church sent us off with an official farewell, speeches, music, poems, flowers and gifts, hundreds of kisses, and many, many tears. We drove to the station past the sawmill, the high school, and the Lutheran church, and I saw my best friend standing by the road with his dog. Yesterday I had pledged my eternal friendship to him. Now he wouldn't even wave. He just patted his dog and walked away, and I was very sad. The train from Schwentainen took us to Ortelsburg, the county seat, where we changed for a train to Allenstein, then changed once more for an express to Berlin.

Our new home was a part of the church building at Boddinstrasse 45 in Neukoelln, just east of the Tempelhof airport. We were so close to the airport that I could see every detail of the low-flying planes as they roared directly over our apartment.

I arrived in this throbbing capital of the Third Reich

wide-eyed and alive to the marching music. Here in the next few years the seeds of Aryan superiority and militarism took root in my young heart, side by side with the gospel of peace and love. Here was the beginning of the battle for my allegiance—a battle that would break into the open only in the last dying and disillusioning days of the war.

III

Deeply involved in reminiscing, I had almost forgotten that I was really in Czechoslovakia and that Mrs. Bata could not stand there for hours doing nothing. I also had some chores to do if I wanted to get a decent noon meal. That was the iron rule at the Villa. Everybody had to do some work during the day to earn the right to eat.

It was my turn that day to clean up the toilet and the washroom. I couldn't understand how just a few boys could make such a mess out of these two rooms, but Juergen, one of my new friends, just laughed. "You wait until all the boys are back. If you think that this is bad, you should see the washroom after all one hundred *Pimpfe* (an official nickname for Hitler Youth members) have washed. And," he complained, "then we have to march again."

"What?" He had caught me off guard. "When do we have to march?"

"Three times a day! Just as we are now walking to the *Volkshaus* for meals, we will march in formation with loud commands and singing."

"You don't like to sing?"

"Sure, but not when snowflakes are flying into my open mouth."

By lunch, I decided that I was sufficiently well again to join the few boys on their way to the Volkshaus. As we walked through the streets, we seemed to blend in with the rest of the population. We had on civilian clothes and no one took special notice of us.

On the way back from lunch we were free to stop at the stores and look around. My ability to speak Czech impressed my friends and the salesgirls. Often the Czechs reached under the counter and produced items otherwise reserved exclusively for their own.

Those two-kilometer walks to the Volkshaus three times a day were our happiest moments. While we waited for the others to return, life at the Villa consisted of trying to avoid Herr Grothe and doing a decent job as he ordered. At night the high iron gate and fence around our park-like garden gave us a feeling of being locked up.

With the chores and the walk back and forth to town, there was little time left for anything else. Of course we could always write a letter home and hand it in to Herr Grothe, unsealed. But the thought that he would read every word of it quickly discouraged that idea.

So I would often just stretch out on my bunk bed and daydream. Since I couldn't imagine what was ahead, I retreated into the past.

I remembered the first day in our apartment in Berlin. We had four rooms, plus a kitchen, a bathroom,

28

and a small utility room. Since we had arrived in October, we didn't find out how cold and dark the apartment was until a few weeks later. As I walked through the empty rooms, wondering how I could ever like living here, a plane thundered over our house. I dashed to the window and there it was, so close I could even see its windows and markings. I had never seen anything like it. But in the streets below children were playing on the cobblestones without bothering to look up. I couldn't understand why they weren't straining to watch every movement of the miracle.

A few months after we arrived in Berlin I started school. Until then our warm and affectionate home life, with its daily prayers and practice of Christian virtues, had shaped most of my thinking. Now the state was to have its chance.

Siegfried had warned me that school was tough and that I wouldn't be able to take it, but I approached it with typical German determination. I'd show him.

Still, I was glad that summer of '39 when we went back to East Prussia. I had missed the trees, the endless landscape, and the barefoot running over dirt and grass. I was almost eight and my grandfather treated me like a man. He needed help in the fields, and he taught me to hold the reins and drive the wagons.

That summer I noticed something in East Prussia that hadn't been there before. The villages were crowded with soldiers and armored vehicles. The final military buildup had begun, although I knew nothing about the impending war at the time. I had heard that the Poles were pushing around the German-speaking peoples in their country, and I had seen newspaper pictures of the horrible things the Poles had done. I had also heard the cry, "an eye for an eye and a tooth for a tooth," and I wondered if that was right. As I remembered my

29

teaching, that was the Old Testament way, not the new way.

Nonetheless, the sight of troops inspired me. I wanted to grow up to be a part of this fearless army. The tanks in particular impressed me, and I imagined myself sitting on top of one of those noisy creeping monsters.

At the end of summer we took the train back to Berlin, and there I first heard the rumor of war. My father had spent several months each year in military training. I knew that he'd have to go if there was a war, and a few doubts began to form in the back of my mind. I was eager to be a soldier myself, but could I ever kill anyone? I, who had always been taught to turn the other cheek and who didn't even know how to defend myself? I, who had learned that I should love my enemies and who cried over my own weakness?

However, war was a way to restore what had been taken from us. Of course I didn't know what it meant that Hitler had "liberated" the Rhineland, then Austria, then the Sudentenland. I only knew that Germany had the best army in the world, and I thrilled when I heard our leaders shout the slogan, *"Deutschland über Alles."* I was proud, but then, hadn't my father taught us, "Revenge is mine. I will repay, saith the Lord"? Was this the way God repaid? Was God going to help us beat the countries that had once beaten us? Deep inside I was just a little frightened and confused.

As school approached in the fall, the older people talked more and more about war. Gasoline rationing began.

On September 1, 1939, at 5:45 A.M., while Berlin roused itself and workers gathered to wait at the newspaper kiosks, German troops crossed the Polish border. *"Der Tag"* had arrived. Suddenly the city went wild. Factories shut down and stores closed. People ran through

30

the streets shouting, and the headlines blazed, "No peace until victory." An order went out on the radio for every family to fly the flag in celebration of the new victorious era.

I was jubilant and raced to the home of one friend after another. We wondered what it would mean for us and if it would last long enough for us to take part. My father had told me that toward the end of World War I no one had thought of going to school, and I was sure that would happen again.

When we discovered flags flying all over the neighborhood, I called to my brother and we took the steps to our apartment two at a time.

"We have to fly the flag," Siegfried panted, and I dashed to the storeroom where I knew it was kept. In wild excitement we hoisted it out the window to become part of the frenzied crowd.

My parents didn't say much. They seemed subdued, a little confused. My mother was sad, and I couldn't understand why, in that glorious hour, they could not join our celebration.

As I had hoped, school was cancelled that day and the next. We listened most of the day as the radio broadcast news of the blitzkrieg. Fifty-six German divisions rumbled toward Warsaw and other Polish cities. The Stuka dive bombers with their nerve-wracking sirens dropped like lightning out of the sky on the Polish troops, and heavier bombers destroyed fortifications and industry.

Meanwhile we went back to school. We had a report card coming in less than a month, but it was hard to concentrate. In school we swapped war stories and photos from magazines and newspapers. We became specialists in the types of planes and armored vehicles and all things military.

Finally on September 27 it ended, and on the next day all Germany celebrated one of the shortest and "most victorious wars," as our teacher called it. In school we were herded into the auditorium where flags, martial music, and speeches gave us the overwhelming assurance that Germany's leadership as the master race was about to begin.

It was several days after that victory celebration that I asked my homeroom teacher, Herr Bendritz, the question that had been troubling me. At the beginning of class I stood and addressed him so that everyone in the second grade could hear.

"Herr Bendritz, why are all the Jews bad?"

A few days before that I had heard the principal call them "the most corrupt and treacherous people in the world." That wasn't the first such talk I'd heard, of course. The National Socialists had made anti-Semitism a mark of the new Germany, and party people outdid themselves to prove their loyalty.

I had been raised on the Old and New Testaments, and characters such as David, Joshua, Peter, and John were my heroes. I had followed Abraham out of Ur and gone down to Egypt with Joseph. I had learned that the Jews were God's chosen people, and I had a friend, Esau, who, while he was nothing out of the ordinary, was still a good kid.

My question caught the teacher by surprise. Why was the pastor's son, who got an A in conduct, asking such a question?

"Because they are Jews," he spluttered.

"But Esau here is a Jew," I pointed to the dark, curly-haired boy beside me, "and he's a good boy."

"All Jews are bad," the teacher replied, his voice slightly louder, "even Esau and the other two Jewish students in this class."

I raised my arm again for permission to answer, but Herr Bendritz fancied himself in the role of an anti-Semite and was just getting started. "The Jews are the reason why your parents had to go through an economic depression. The Jews are the reason Germany lost the last war."

I'm sure most of the second grade would have been happy to return to spelling and reading, but the teacher, a member of the Nazi Party, continued his tirade, waving his arms and shouting.

"Every good German has to hate the Jews. They poison the pure Aryan blood. They're dangerous bloodsuckers. They undermine the economy. Boys, do not mix with Jews. The fatherland needs you unpolluted from the stench of this inferior race."

It was the stock party line—right out of *Mein Kampf.*

After school I wanted to see Esau, to reassure him that he was still my friend. But with Herr Bendritz watching, I was afraid to stop, so I walked quickly past his desk, avoiding his dark, sad eyes.

At home I went directly to my father's study, burst in and related to him the entire incident. "I don't believe all that he said," I concluded, "but he really got mad at me."

My ever-patient father had heard it all before, of course, and he knew that the constant barrage of lies, half-truths, and accusations could turn around the most rational mind. He would not attack the attackers, however. He would use only the truth of the Word as his weapon, so he carefully reviewed for me the history which I'd heard many times.

As he finished the story of the Jewish race and God's leading of them, he reminded me, "Don't ever forget, Reini, Jesus was a Jew. So were Mary and Joseph and all the disciples."

I couldn't get the topic out of my head that night, and the next day I determined to ask Herr Bendritz one more question. I raised my hand at the beginning of class, but he ignored me and began calling the roll. When he called my name, I replied, "Present, and I have one more question!"

"What's it about?" he asked sharply.

"About the Jews, Sir." But I was beginning to doubt the wisdom of what I was going to do.

"We discussed that yesterday," he dismissed the topic and continued calling the roll.

I remained standing, however.

"What is it, Kerstan? Why are you standing?"

"Because I have one more question about the Jews."

His face turned red but he controlled his temper.

"Ja, ja, what do you want to know?"

"Last year my father took me into the business section of Berlin."

I hesitated but Herr Bendritz impatiently urged me on.

"We passed a synagogue that was burning, but nobody was trying to put the fire out. When my father inquired why, he was told, 'We don't waste water on Jews except to drown them.' "

The teacher was shifting from one foot to the other, so I hurried on.

"When we came to the Berliner Strasse, many of the stores were on fire, and there were slogans on the walls—'We don't buy from Jewish rats' and 'Jews out.' "

"Ah," the teacher now broke into my report, "look at the genius we have here! Last year he was only six years old and could not read, but now he claims he read all of the graffiti. Tell me, how did you know what was painted on the windows of the stores?"

"My father read it to me," I said, now close to tears.

"So your father read it to you. And what else did he do? Did he like the slogans? What did he say?"

"No, father was very sad and upset. He likes the Jews, because all the Apostles were Jews . . . and even Jesus was a Jew," I quickly threw in so as to impress the teacher.

But Mr. Bendritz was not impressed. He closed the roll book, leaned back in his chair, looked out of the window, then at me, then again out of the window.

"Yes, the *Kristallnacht*, I remember it well. Our party troop was called out to special duty."

He began to reminisce.

"We were to bring paint, brushes, hammers, and matches. We knew exactly where the Jews had their stores, and we knew where they met on the Sabbath. So we went to work. We painted those slogans and broke the locks, but we did not loot."

"But all the windows were broken, and many people were taking things out of the stores without paying for them. I saw them," I countered.

Mr. Bendritz seemed to make a mental note, probably not to give an A in conduct to a boy who had the audacity to challenge his purifying action during the Kristallnacht.

"The party members would never stoop to such a low level, not even towards Jews. After we had marked the Jewish property, we went home." He was slightly indignant.

Now my classmates came alive.

"And who burned the synagogue?" they asked, fascinated by the story.

"Well, on the way home we took care of that, too, but we made sure first that there were no people in the synagogue."

On the way home from school, my friends and I

35

talked about that night. We all remembered it. Some of them, in fact, had brought home loot.

"My father took a watch from a Jewish jeweler's shop," Juergen told us. I looked at him in surprise.

"Why not?" he continued. "My father said that the Jews are stealing it from other merchants in the first place."

Some of the other boys proudly reported that they had thrown stones at the shop windows, and the police had not interfered. I felt left out. My father had walked with me through the chaos, but he had not taken a single piece of the merchandise littering the streets and store windows, nor had he permitted me to pick up anything. He had just walked in disbelief and said over and over again, "Oh, no, they should not have touched God's people. This is going to have a bad ending."

At the same time he must have suspected that this was only a beginning.

IV

Service to the Reich was an honor. Every German tried to believe it, wanted to believe it, even though it meant sacrifice and hardship at times. Everything went for the war effort. Food ration cards gave us limited supplies of butter, meat, bread. Gas was rationed, soap hard to get. Everywhere the signs of the shopkeepers repeated *Ausverkauft*—Sold out. At night there was the blackout and always there was the motto, "One Folk, One Reich, One Fuehrer"—we heard it many times.

So it should have been no surprise when my father was drafted on November 2, 1939, ten days before my eighth birthday.

At eighteen, young men and women left the Hitler Youth for the *Arbeitsdienst,* the Labor Service. Military service followed that. It was, as Hitler had written in *Mein Kampf,* "the crowning point of a citizen's education." My mother had hoped that because he was a pastor my father would not have to go, but there were no exceptions.

She took it hard, crying most of the days he was preparing to leave. He wanted to leave the congregation in good hands, so he arranged for lay preachers and gave my mother instructions on what to do in various situations.

I tried to comfort my mother, but she was not the stereotype of a stoical German woman. I was proud of my father and couldn't believe he'd be in danger. Besides, though I didn't tell this to anyone at the time, now, when people asked, I could tell them my father was a soldier, not a pastor. It was hard enough to be a Christian at times, but being the son of a pastor was much more difficult.

Several days before Christmas Father came home on leave. It's hard to describe how we felt because Christmas is such a special time in Germany. The government relaxed food rations and gave a special bonus on Christmas week. We could get an extra egg, a little extra sugar, and chocolate and spices.

My brother and I had already gone to buy the tree—"A very beautiful tree," my father complimented us.

But then he took over his role as head of the family. We were not allowed to get even a glance of what was going on in the living room on the day before Christmas. We could hear the rustling of paper and we tried to peek through the keyhole. Occasionally my father would come out and suggest that we make the time go faster by singing Christmas carols. We sang our hearts out, but the hands on the clock just did not seem to move.

Then at exactly five o'clock the door opened, as it did

each year, and, to the sounds of Christmas music from the radio, we stepped into the decorated room. We could look at the gifts under the Christmas tree, but we couldn't touch them yet. First Father read the original Christmas story from the Bible. Then we prayed and each family member took part. Next Father would call out the names of relatives, and at each mention of a name either he or one of us children would light a candle until the entire room was brightly lit with candles on the Christmas tree and all over the room.

Even on this wartime Christmas Eve we had gifts. Siegfried and I were soon busy trying out new toys and examining the other gifts, but our parents were quiet. Something seemed to dampen the joy that usually filled the house on the holidays. It was, we knew, the knowledge that in a few days Father would leave us again, and this time he would probably be sent to the Front. I didn't know exactly what it meant to be at war with Great Britain and France and that a month before Christmas Russian troops had invaded Finland. I could sense the seriousness of it, however, as I watched my parents, and it alarmed me.

On January 30, 1940, Father left for France.

The following summer he came home on furlough, but he lacked our enthusiasm for the war, and that disappointed me. I was, more than just on the surface, a thoroughly indoctrinated product of the party propaganda system. In school, from the radio, from my friends, and, it seemed, from the spirit of the air around me, I absorbed the tenets of the German religion—faith in Germany itself.

But there was always the small voice of doubt, weak but never completely silent. Father was grateful that he hadn't had to fire a shot. Could he not kill the enemy because of his Christian beliefs? And, as much

39

as I wanted to be a soldier, could *I* pull the trigger?

For the most part, however, these two areas of my life,—my love for Jesus Christ and the church, and my pride in the Third Reich—occupied two separate compartments in my mind and my life.

"Hitler has said that in two more months he will march into London," Siegfried boasted to my father.

"I sure hope so, but I doubt it," father answered.

"Do you know what Churchill told his people?" my brother went on? "He said he could offer nothing but blood, toil, tears, and sweat."

"And Hermann Goering said he will change his name to Meier if even one foreign airplane should fly over German territory."

"I sure hope so, I sure hope so," my father said, leaving it to our imagination whether he hoped for no planes over Germany or for Goering to change his name to Meier.

Our *Deutscher Kleinempfaenger* stood on a small shelf in the kitchen. For obvious reasons the party wanted each household to have this small radio, and it was often the center of attention. We gathered around it to hear the voice of Joseph Goebbels, the propaganda minister, or to hear the Fuehrer himself. In front of its speaker I had listened entranced to Baldur von Schirach, the top Nazi Youth leader. It was constantly broadcasting, a part of the scene like the wallpaper, something that was all around us and that we took for granted.

Through the radio we had learned about Germany's liberation of one neighborhood state after another, and now we listened intently for news of the war. I believed, through the half truths and twisted lies on the radio, that the Allies employed every dirty trick they knew. The radio would not stop telling us over and over again how criminal were the British, or how weak and sneaky were the French, or how strong and superior were the Germans. And, in between, the Berlin Symphony played the great music of the German composers.

I could hardly keep my mind on studying in those days. I managed to upgrade my C in music, but my B in conduct attested to my interest in the war on the Western Front. At home I studied the map, following the troops into Denmark and Norway, then Belgium and Holland, and finally France. I gulped up every war booklet I could find and read my father's letters over and over. When we heard of the shameful evacuation of British, Belgian, and French troops at Dunkerque, we knew that the German nation was truly a superior race. "Destiny" and "Fate" were two of Adolf Hitler's favorite words, and these forces, I believed, drove us to accomplish more than any other nation in history.

That summer we again went to East Prussia for our vacation. It was a beautiful feeling to drive through the former Polish Corridor, knowing that this was now part of the German Reich. No Polish soldiers locked the doors of the trains as they had before, and the swastika flew in each village.

While we were there, however, British planes penetrated German antiaircraft defenses and raided German cities. Goering, for all I knew, had not changed his name, but I wanted to be back in Berlin. Siegfried and I had long discussions while in bed. We imagined the enemy planes approaching, the noise of the bombs, the light from the shelling, and we were disappointed to miss it all. When we did get back, it was a letdown that our entire district was undamaged.

One day father came home on his weekend leave quite disturbed. At the evening meal he told us that Hitler had offered Great Britain a negotiated peace, but the British had not even replied. My father was deeply

41

disappointed in the British.

"Now the war is going to draw on," he said, "and I will have to serve much longer."

Imbued with the spirit of the war, as only a child can be, and soaking up the militant exhortations of the state like a sponge, I was ready for the war to go on. I wanted to experience it myself.

I didn't have to wait long.

All the houses in Berlin had converted their basements to air aid shelters. Workers had put in extra support pillars and had broken through the foundations between houses to provide an escape if one house was hit.

I was asleep one night when the siren sounded, and I groped my way to the basement behind my mother. The other residents had outfitted the shelter with armchairs, blankets, emergency equipment, and drinking water.

That first night was a false alarm. After several hours we went back upstairs.

But a few nights later the real thing came. From then on, several nights a week we were herded into the shelter while the British bombers flew overhead. In the daytime we searched the streets for shell splinters and swapped them the way other kids would swap baseball cards.

As the air raids became more frequent, the government instituted an evacuation program, the *Kinder-Land-Verschickung* (KLV; Evacuation of Children to Rural Areas).Siegfried was sent to Weisswasser, about 150 kilometers southeast of Berlin, and suddenly I realized how much he had meant to me. Although he had spent more time studying in the past year, while I was roaming the streets playing war games, I now felt, in a small way, another loss to the war. First my father, now Siegfried. When we went off again for the summer to East

Prussia, the enemy was getting closer.

That fall I was inducted into the German Youth. Few events in the life of a German boy could mean as much as this. Even before they had come to power the National Socialists had organized youth. In *Mein Kampf* Hitler had outlined a Spartan-type training program for the young, beginning very early in life. It was the duty of the state to provide physical as well as mental education, and, by feeding the spirit as well, to produce virtues such as loyalty, the will to sacrifice, and self-mastery.

At ten I could join the first phase of the program, the German Youth, and at fourteen I would graduate to the Hitler Youth. I had looked forward to it for as long as I could remember.

At the end of 1941, a few days after my tenth birthday, my mother took me to register, and I received a list of uniform items to buy. Several days after that, I stood with dozens of other boys in a large square, and a youth leader pronounced us official members.

It wasn't until a week later, however, that I had the first indication of conflict between my love for all things German and my love for Jesus Christ. I was ordered to appear in a huge square in Neukoelln along with hundreds of other boys and girls. No civilians were allowed. We stood shoulder to shoulder in long rows, eyes straight ahead, while band music and fanfares brought on one of the high-ranking Hitler Youth leaders.

I remember the day vividly, and I was close to tears. They broke us up into smaller units to administer the oath, and I had begun to say the words along with the others, when we came to the phrase, "I pledge my life and blood to the one who leads us all." I had pledged my life once before, to Jesus Christ, and at ten years old I understood enough to know that no man here on earth could usurp that place. I could have no higher commander. Frightened that I would be caught, nevertheless I stopped speaking when I came to those words.

It left me confused and shaken, but I never did tell my parents. Even then I was beginning to believe what I had heard the youth leaders say—you can never trust your parents all the way. Some things you have to keep to yourself.

V

With typical German punctuality, the hop-picking crew returned on the day scheduled. Now I'd find out what life at our *Kinder-Land-Verschickung* camp in Czechoslovakia was really like. Herr Grothe ordered us to put on our brown shirts and full uniforms and wait outside for him. We talked and laughed while we waited, anticipating the return of our friends.

Suddenly Herr Grothe stormed out, red-faced and shouting, "You no-good, undisciplined punks. Who told you to stand around like a bunch of sick Jews? Is that the way you thank me for letting you have all this freedom?"

He seemed close to tears, gasping for breath like a madman, and I had my first inkling of what was to come. The quiet nights in the big, empty room and the easy, relaxed days puttering around the Villa were over. They had given me a chance to sort things out, to look back and trace my short life up to the present and to gain some perspective for the days ahead as a German Youth away from home.

As we marched to the train station, we must have presented a laughable picture to the Czechs—a dozen young boys in uniform, lead by a puffing, indignant civilian who knew little about marching and military commands. We reached the old brick station just as the train came to a halt and sixty or more tanned and ragged hop pickers descended on·us. While Herr Grothe fumed, they broke into our formation, greeted old friends, slapped backs, and shouted to each other. One boy, however, stood out from the crowd. He was dressed in full uniform, and he stood stiffly, looked around, then walked in exaggerated fashion up to Herr Grothe and saluted. I had been warned about Kurt. Although not much older than we were, he was one of thousands of boys from all over Germany chosen to be part of an elite corps. They were, supposedly, physically perfect specimens of sound Germanic stock who had great zeal for Nazi ideals. They would become the new aristocracy that would some day lead the Third Reich. At first they were sent to Adolf Hitler Schools, but with the drain of manpower during the war they were pulled out for more practical service.

Kurt became our platoon leader.

"Achtung!" The command boomed over the disorderly scene. Instantly the uniformed and the ununiformed lined up at attention. Then, while Kurt smartly called cadence and the townspeople stared grimly, we marched back over the cobblestone streets to the villa.

Kurt was just hitting his stride. As we passed the hotel across from the station where the older classes were housed, he ordered us to sing, but since he couldn't sing himself, he relied·on us. We began a well-known marching song but it died almost instantly in a wave of laughter.

Kurt was furious. "I'm going to get you pigs now," he shouted.

We tried a second time but the same thing happened, and Kurt raged and swore at us. He was obviously frustrated and embarrassed because of the Czechs on the sidewalk who were trying to hide their laughter.

Next it was Herr Grothe's turn for a temper tantrum. He had gone on ahead, and as we arrived Kurt halted the platoon and turned us to face the camp leader. For a long moment Herr Grothe said nothing. His chest heaved as he tried to compose himself. Then he began slowly, sneering, "And where, my lords, is the luggage?" He always called us "my lords" when he was angry—which was quite often. "Have you hired slaves to bring it to you while you rest?"

We realized then that, in our zeal to please our platoon leader, we had forgotten the knapsacks. We were a keyed-up, exuberant group that day, and once more we exploded in laughter.

"Don't laugh at me." Herr Grothe's face turned red. "You sick Jews, you'll pay for your forgetfulness." And he went on with his tirade.

It was a portentous, if not frightening, beginning, for this was to be a daily occurrence—the browbeating, the screaming, the contempt of the short Nazi school teacher and the tall thin German Youth leader.

Something else happened that day that should have warned me of things to come. While we cleaned up the washrooms with the returnees, one boy stopped me.

"Aren't you Reinhold, the preacher's kid from Neukoelln?"

I recognized him as Wolfgang, one of the boys from my school in Berlin. He had made great sport out of my being a Baptist pastor's son.

"Hey, guys, meet Reinhold the Baptist. He likes water. Let's baptize the Baptist." He had hardly said it before he let his bucket fly at me. Another one followed and then another, but I hardly noticed them. It was the first one that was the slap in the face. Of all the boys in Berlin, why did Wolfgang have to be here? He had been the leader, the loudest of a gang that constantly mocked my Christian faith, and I wished for a moment he had been killed by a bomb in Berlin. But it was worse than I thought at first. A half hour later when I had finished cleaning the washroom and returned to the dormitory, it was Wolfgang again who greeted me.

"Boys," he turned to the room, and introduced me to the other ten boys there. "This is Reinhold, our newly rebaptized roommate."

My heart dropped. Back in Berlin I could go home after school and get away from Wolfgang and his type. Here I'd have to live with them, twenty-four hours a day. It was too much. I fought back the tears, pulled myself out of my wet clothes and threw myself on my bed.

I was beginning to have doubts about the war and about myself. I wished desperately to be with my mother or father, but I had no idea whether I'd ever see them again, or even if they were still alive. Had my great adventure come to a miserable and inglorious end?

With the entire school together, Herr Grothe reintroduced traditional Prussian discipline. We stood in formation at least half an hour before we marched off to the dining room for our meals. We wore clean uniforms and had our hair neatly trimmed.

Herr Grothe read out the rules. "We will hoist the flag every morning and you will all be there. When we walk we will march. When we march we will sing. When we eat there will be no talking. You will have classes in the morning, and in the afternoon you will have four hours of study. Saturday afternoons are free."

He didn't mention Sunday. That was his time to surprise us with movies, botany excursions, visits from party members, or other not-so-glamorous forms of entertainment.

It was, in short, a highly regimented life designed to toughen mind and body. Herr Grothe was the unquestioned authority, and Kurt stood ready to carry out his every command—even to add a few of his own. They proudly wore their swastika pins on their lapel, and we wore our German Youth version of it, in uniform or out.

After a few weeks in camp, I noticed that there was never enough food to overcome my hunger. In the morning we had two small slices of rye bread, at noon soup or potatoes with gravy, or occasionally some meat on Sunday, and bread again in the evening. That might have been all right. In the fifth year of the war no one expected a board flowing with sausage and dumplings and pastries. But as we were leaving the dining hall we noticed that the teachers often slipped into the kitchen to secrete extra provisions off to their rooms.

One day I decided I'd write home about this injustice. There were only two other boys in the room at the time, and I felt secure enough to write what I wanted, thinking that I'd smuggle the letter out into the village post office. Herr Grothe read all of our regularly sent mail "for security reasons."

After a few introductory remarks I wrote, "Don't feel badly if you don't have enough to eat. We have very little here. But while our rations are getting smaller and smaller, and the quality worse, the teachers' food seems to be getting better and better."

49

"Well, Reinhold, I'm glad you're writing a letter." Herr Grothe suddenly loomed over my shoulder, and I spun around at the same time trying to cover my letter with my arm.

He spoke in the syrupy-kind voice he often used on me. I found it embarrassing, and it further alienated me from the other boys. When he came into our room in the morning, he'd yell, "Get up you lazy good-for-nothings . . . get up." Then he'd lean over my bed and say sweetly, "How about getting up, Reinhold? It's such a nice day."

It made me burn, and soon as he went out, someone would mimic him, "Reinhold, dear, won't you please get up, Reinhold—if you don't mind."

"Let me see your letter," he asked, smiling down at me. He had no idea, of course, what I was writing, as he reached for the paper.

I was horrified. I stared at him, then in unheard-of defiance, I stammered, "No!"

Herr Grothe stared back, unbelieving. His forehead creased and he asked calmly, "No?" Then more loudly, "No?"

Suddenly he reached for the paper and snarled, "Give me that!"

He snatched, but I held on, fully aware that I was in deep trouble no matter who got the letter. The sheet ripped as he pulled, and he grinned and held up his half in his hand. But the smile faded slowly as he read.

I glanced at my half, the top, and read, ". . . while our rations are getting smaller and smaller. . . ." He had the rest of the sentence, and I knew he could guess what went before.

His eyes went wide as he read, and he fought for control. "You little . . . how dare you . . . you. . . ." His dried-out form shook. "Get out . . . get out." He pointed

50

toward the door and leaned threateningly toward me.

Out in the cold hall he ordered me to take off my shoes and socks and stand at attention saluting.

"Stand there until you faint," he yelled, adding a string of curses. "You'll get no supper and no sleep if I can help it. I'll teach you."

Still shaking his head, he stomped into his own room across the hall, and I could hear him continuing his tirade, telling his wife about the insolent pastor's son.

For the moment I felt only relief that he was gone. Although I knew I had a long night ahead, it might, I thought at the time, have been worse. It was a stupid thing to do, but I didn't regret it. I felt only a perverse sort of pride in showing him and his staff that we knew. Now they knew we knew.

On their way to supper, my roommates had to pass me. They didn't laugh, nor did they show any sign of sympathy, at least outwardly. But suddenly I felt a kinship with them. I was no longer Herr Grothe's "dear Reinhold." I had become a victim of his wrath and thus one of them. For the moment I didn't feel the cold that had been creeping up through my bare feet. Even when Frau Grothe on her way past wrapped her coat around her bulging body and looked at me in disgust, I stood with my shoulders squared, not moving a breath.

"That malicious monster, I'll tame him. That sniveling preacher's kid." I could hear Herr Grothe complaining to her.

When they had all gone to supper, I hurriedly slipped into my room, changed into a heavier shirt, and rubbed my feet until the blood started circulating again. On an impulse I grabbed my father's most recent letter and took it with me back to the hall. Then I took up a post by the window where I could see anyone returning to the house.

It was early November, and harsh winds had already stripped the trees. A few snowflakes tried unsuccessfully to cover the round, and the big, empty house conspired to turn my pride into loneliness. I began to read my father's letter, searching for the warmth and charm that they always gave off.

My father filled his letters with biblical quotations, and I read every word of them this time, craving the comfort which seemed to come from both my father and from God. "Take no thought for the morrow." "Stand firm." "In everything give thanks." "I will never leave you nor forsake you."

I was lost in thought when the door banged open and the boys, back from supper, barged up the steps. I quickly resumed my saluting stance just before Herr Grothe came in. He came puffing up the stairway and pointed a finger in my face.

"Well, have you had enough time to think about your sins? You should know all about sin."

I didn't know what to say, so I kept quiet.

"Too good to talk to me, huh? Well, I'll teach you a lesson you won't forget for a long time," and with that he turned his back and disappeared into his room.

Hours later, he passed me on his curfew-inspection rounds without saying a word. By that time the heavier shirt was useless against the penetrating cold and my feet had almost lost their feeling. As he returned to his room, he stopped and looked at me. "I hope you freeze to death," he hissed. "Dead people don't need food."

His intense hatred chilled me even more, and I knew that the long shivering night ahead was not the worst I'd have to face. The past, however, was all I could cling to for the moment, and it helped keep my mind off the numbing cold. I remembered the winter I had spent in East Prussia as part of the evacuation program for endangered cities. It was a strange, almost unreal lull in the storm of war. Deep in snow-covered country, we spent the days on the countless trivial tasks of existence, with little time to think about world-shaking events so many miles away.

I thought about the snow removal parties we'd been subjected to in Berlin. The Nazi party had extended its control of German life to every city block. A party member, called the "block warden," not only supplied his people with ration cards but also kept a watchful eye on every activity. He was the only man in the neighborhood who greeted everyone with "Heil Hitler." One day he knocked at our door and ordered us to join our fellow citizens in their snow removal efforts.

"Comrades," he greeted the women and children gathered there, "I am glad that you have come on your own to contribute your time and energy to the task. Your husbands and fathers would have done it but they are defending our glorious Fatherland. We are one nation. Our Fuehrer is proud that. . . ."

I wondered if all block wardens were such pompous fools.

It was past 2:30 A.M. when Herr Grothe stuck his head out of the door. The hall was dark, and I heard him swear and mumble. "Where is he?"

"I'm here, Sir."

"Oh, there you are."

He had been drinking and after he'd had a few, he often swore—a practice strictly forbidden to his charges. He came close to me and put his hand on my shoulder, but then, remembering the changed circumstances, he hastily withdrew it and straightened up.

"You stupid boy. How could you do such a thing? Don't you know we're all starving?"

He raised his voice, "We are one folk and one nation.

We have to stick together. Remember, the Fuehrer has not enough to eat."

He was close to tears.

"I hate this place. I hate this camp. I hate to be hated by the Czechs. I hate you all."

He had started out sounding like the block warden but ended more like a homesick camp kid. I had no pity for him. Through a crack in the polished veneer of racial superiority I had caught a glimpse of the weakness underneath. A child quickly senses hypocrisy, and at that moment I lost whatever respect I ever had for Herr Grothe.

"Go to bed, you no-good preacher's brat," he yelled at me as he went to his own room. He didn't have to yell. I ran for the warmth of the room and my bed and flung myself in it.

A strange aftermath of the incident came that next morning when the boys crowded around me wanting to know what it was like. Wolfgang, my tormentor, and the least sympathetic if not the most hostile one in the room, handed me a piece of his highly treasured chocolate. It was a surprising and moving act of friendship, and the slogan I had heard so often, "One folk, one nation," sprang to mind. The sustenance I'd earlier received from my father's letter and from my own faith was far from my thinking now. I grasped the very real offer of fellowship in an earthly circle and said silently, "Our leaders were right, we're one room, one team, one camp, and one German people."

VI

In December of that year German troops in Belgium, wearing captured American uniforms and riding in American jeeps, cut communication lines, turned around signposts, marked nonexistent mine fields and generally caused confusion for the Allied armies. In the hilly wooded area of the Ardennes, the Germans threw twenty divisions against four of the Americans, pushed them back and caused what has become known as "The Battle of the Bulge."

It was Hitler's last major offensive, a clever strategic move, aided by bad weather, in which he drew on every man, tank, and bullet he had available to his collapsing war machine. It wasn't enough, however, and by Christmas Day the Allies had called up reserves and were moving toward the German border again.

We knew, of course, that the Allies had landed the

previous summer and that we were fighting in France. No system of propaganda can keep that type of information from the people.

Off in Czechoslovakia in our small villa, however, we knew very little about the real situation and heard only that "the Fatherland was getting ready for its final victory." That was why we couldn't go home for Christmas.

Kurt called us out to the drive and we stood in formation while he read the directive from Berlin.

"German boys, I am proud of your faith in Germany. We need the cooperation of both the home front and the battle front. The words of our field marshal, Hermann Goering, 'Guns instead of butter,' have taken hold in your hearts. I also want you to remember the slogan that is painted on just about every locomotive: 'Wheels must roll for victory.' You will therefore stay at your respective places without coming home. You will bear the sacrifice of being away from home longer than intended because Germany needs every single wheel to transport soldiers and guns.

"Not long ago railroad wheels were transporting many happy young people as part of my 'Strength Through Joy' program. Now all of us will have to put aside recreation and personal demands in order to make the final victory possible.

"I order you therefore to give up your right to vacation transportation. Have a good time during the Christmas season, when we observe, as our Germanic forefathers did many thousand years ago, the change of the sun constellation, when the nights are getting shorter and the days longer."

That came as a blow, but at the time I probably didn't realize how much I needed to be with my family again, to go to church, celebrate the birth of Christ, sing and pray and rejoice together with them. My Christian life had been slowly smothered in the suffocating camp environment. I no longer read my Bible, no longer prayed each day. Our family had been very close, and I ached for the warm circle of Christian love that had permeated our home. But because we did it for the Fuehrer and the Fatherland, it did not seem to be a sacrifice.

We looked forward to Easter, therefore, hoping, expecting that we'd have a holiday then. This time there was no special word from the Fuehrer, only Herr Grothe's grumbling, "Sorry, boys, the country still needs the wheels for victory. However," he added, arrogantly, "I will see to it that Easter will be a worthy occasion."

We knew Herr Grothe's worthy occasions. Some of them had already bored us to death.

I was depressed for several days before Easter. Then rainy weather set in to make things worse. I moped around, thinking about Easter in our church. My father always had some special way of making it a joyful time. I wondered if anyone would be there at all. Probably just a few older folks.

"You think they'll let us go to church here?" I asked the boys at breakfast.

They looked at me as though I'd gone crazy. For one thing, we weren't even safe on the streets during the daytime unless we had four or more together. Gangs of Czechs had mutilated and even murdered Hitler Youth they had found alone.

Marching back to the Villa, we passed many Czechs dressed in their Easter attire. I usually resented the disgust and hate I found on their faces, but that morning I understood. We shattered the quiet beauty of an Easter Sunday morning with our marching and our loud, cliché-ridden German Youth songs. Somewhere inside me a seed of rebellion began to take root.

In front of the Villa before he dismissed us, Herr Grothe's whistle cut into our conversation. "Now hear this, my friends." He paused for a moment to give his announcement weight.

"Today is Easter, as you all know. To brighten up this year's festivities, our Fuehrer"—at the mention of his name, Herr Grothe drew himself up to his tallest height—"has presented us with a special film, 'Quex, Hitler's Young Man.' "

We stifled a groan. It was an old film about a boy who had pledged his life to Hitler but had been murdered by the communists. We'd all seen it several times.

But Herr Grothe wasn't through.

"Platoon leader Kurt will also tell you about church youth organizations and lodges and why Hitler has prohibited them. Then we will have single-dish lunch to honor our heroic soldiers who have had nothing but a single dish for many years."

That was a laugh. We'd been having one-dish meals for a long time, too. But I didn't feel like laughing. I felt a sudden surge of anger, and another sprout grew in that seed of rebellion.

As soon as Kurt dismissed us, I raced for the auditorium and started putting chairs on top of the tables.

"What in the world are you doing, Reini?"

Richard and Juergen thought I'd gone crazy, and I wasn't quite sure myself what I was doing.

"C'mon, give me a hand," I shouted without stopping my work.

"Okay, but tell us what it's all about."

"Well, since today is Easter, we're going to have church right here."

"Oh, no! We don't go to church!" And they both stopped working.

I had worked myself into a frenzy by this time, and I

urged them on. "We're going to have a great time, you'll see."

I didn't see the boys arrive myself, but in a few minutes we had some fifty boys, caught up in the game and sitting on the chairs on the tables. The last ones to come in missed the whole point about this being an Easter congregation, but they joined in the fun nevertheless.

"*Achtung!*"

Herr Grothe entered the room and one of the boys instinctively shouted the command. Normally we'd all jump to attention, but this time, for some unknown reason, we sat there, defying him, on strike. Either the others shared the same deep resentment I felt or they were blindly following the leader. Whatever the reason, Herr Grothe fixed us with an icy stare, and Kurt stood a few paces behind him staring at us.

"So, my lords, you have your own plans for today. Is this some kind of a joke? Or are you on strike?"

By then I knew that I'd misled the group. I'd incited a riot and we'd have to pay.

"Down with you," Herr Grothe thundered, but no one moved.

We had never before heard of German Youth defying an order, but here was a whole group of them, in uniform and in rebellion.

Herr Grothe's neck turned red and his face drained pale while he tried a different approach.

"Werner, come forward."

Werner, the class president, jumped from the table and stood before the camp director.

"Tell me, Werner, what is going on?"

"Nothing, Sir!"

"Nothing? Did you hear that, Kurt. The entire camp sits on the tables and he says nothing's going on!"

Without warning, Herr Grothe slapped Werner four times across the face. He wore a steel brace on his hand where he had been wounded in World War I, and he used that on Werner.

At that point the strange scene turned to a nightmare. Kurt stepped forward and began yanking boys and chairs off the table. We all scrambled down and quickly fell into formation. Herr Grothe ordered Kurt to "take these striking communists into the street and teach them some manners," and he marched us out.

We had put on our best uniforms for Easter, and now Kurt marched us through the mud puddles, then made us roll in them. He raged and yelled at us while we splashed each other until every inch of clothing and skin was muddy.

It took us hours to clean up. Then Kurt called us back to the auditorium for the film.

Our one consolation was that there was no time left for Kurt's political training. Although I had managed to have at least this part of the program cancelled, I felt no great victory or triumph. I felt only an inner satisfaction that we had survived the punishment, that we had taken all that Herr Grothe and Kurt could measure out without whimpering. We had proved our toughness. The Fuehrer had said we should be "tough as leather, hard as Krupp's steel, and fast as a greyhound."

Perhaps it really didn't matter if we went to church. Easter, our youth leaders told us, was the time of new life in nature. Well, we were Germany's new, young life. We were the celebration. The world would know that we were ready to take over.

By now I had completely forgotten the embarrassing street scene of that morning when the Czechs scowled at us. On the return to the Villa from dinner, I picked up my feet, stuck my chin out, and joined wholeheartedly in singing:

> The morbid bones of the world
> Are shaking in view of the great war.
> We have conquered the fear;
> for us it has been a great victory.
> We will march on
> until everything will tumble to pieces.
> Today only Germany belongs to us,
> But tomorrow we'll own the whole world.

VII

That unusual Easter was one more proof that there was no room for God in our camp. There was no room for Bible reading or prayer or any other form of religion. But as hard as I tried to make the boys forget that my father was a pastor, they wouldn't.

When I received a letter from my father, they wanted to know how much of the Bible he had quoted. I had once made the mistake of leaving his letter on my bed, and when I returned they mockingly quoted it back to me. I resented it, but nothing I did or didn't do would make them let up.

I don't know where they got the idea, but one afternoon they decided to give me "Holy Communion." Strong hands grabbed me and spread me out on the table in our room. One boy stood by the door to prevent sudden visitors from coming in, and another held a wine bottle filled with water. One more had a few slices of bread. Soon they looked for another thrill.

"Let's make him our official camp chaplain."

"No, we will put him in a manger and feed him with milk like a little baby."

"Let's crucify him!" It was Wolfgang again.

"Yeah, that's good, let's crucify him."

"Crucify, crucify him," I heard all around me.

I had borne the first indignity without a word. Perhaps if I was tough enough they'd finally forget this business and accept me into the group. But crucifixion? The wild look on Wolfgang's face frightened me. I felt he was capable of real harm, and I thought he might have it in for me for the Easter incident.

First they stripped my shirt off. "Jesus didn't have pants on," Richard argued, making himself the specialist in biblical matters.

"That's right. Down with his pants."

"Does anybody have a loin cloth?"

"His underpants will do."

"Wasn't Jesus nailed to the cross?"

My heart almost stopped. They would be crazy enough to use nails.

But the government drive, "Guns instead of butter," was not only an excuse for giving us no butter, it also swallowed up every bit of iron and steel, including nails. Finally they found a rope that would do the job.

"What else did they do to Jesus?" they asked Richard, who was enjoying his role as authority. Apparently he'd been an altar boy at one time.

I looked at Richard and saw him hesitating. "They sp. . . ." He stopped.

"They what?"

"They . . . ah . . . slapped him in the face."

That was all the gang needed. They tied me to the

bunk bed, arms and legs spread out, and each one slapped me. It hurt, of course, but at the time I thought more about that small sign of friendship from Richard. He had been about to say that the mob spit on Jesus, but he changed it. I tried to thank him with a look, but he turned away.

Suddenly Kurt's whistle blew for dinner. In seconds my ten roommates had dashed out the door, leaving me tied up. I don't know what made Herr Grothe look in the room, but suddenly he stood there laughing, slowly at first, then harder and harder until his body shook all over.

I looked down to see myself through Herr Grothe's eyes. I felt naked and ashamed, the object of a dirty joke. Quickly freeing one hand, I held it in front of my briefs. If I had hoped for understanding from him, however, I was to be disappointed. To add to my humiliation, he ordered me to stay in the Villa and miss supper. "It's too late. The others have left." He looked back to take in the scene once more, evidently enjoying it, then slammed the door behind him.

First rage, then helplessness, then self pity swept over me. I fumbled with the knots that held me, on the verge of sobbing, but held it in check. Can a German boy ever weep? Anger mixed with other emotions. Was there no room for all the emotions I felt? Jesus wept, didn't he? I wondered if he had cried at his crucifixion, and if they had been tears of pain or shame. At the same time I realized, ironically, that Jesus would not do well as a German boy today.

I struggled free of my bonds and, as I thought about Jesus' crucifixion, almost involuntarily dropped to my knees beside the bed and pushed my face down into my hands. It had been a long time since I had taken that position, a long time since I had bowed my head or my heart, except for a passing prayer, and really talked to God. I had been taught that Jesus had suffered and died on the cross. I had believed it even though I had not fully grasped it. But now I had suffered, innocently. I had been the object of ridicule without cause.

Suddenly it struck me—He had suffered righteously. He had lived the perfect life, but they had spit on him and nailed him up. But I was faking Christianity. I had given up on even the outward forms. I had stopped praying, stopped reading the Bible, stopped trying to live a Christian life. Now I heard myself pour out my thoughts to God.

"Lord Jesus, my friends think I'm holy, that I believe in you and love you, that I trust you. But you know my heart. You know how I've pushed you out of my life, neglected to read your Word, not stopped to listen to your voice. How foolish it is to be persecuted for a faith that I don't have.

"I want to tell you that I'm sorry. You know I'm not holy. I'm not any better than any boy in this camp.

"But, Lord . . . Lord . . . let my faith grow again. Let it be strong. If I suffer, let it be for a reason—because I love you and do your will."

It felt good to pray again. From now on I'd kneel each evening. Let the insults and the shoes fly around my head. If they wanted to mock me, they'd have a reason.

"Lord, let my new-found zeal outmatch their contempt for you."

VIII

As the allies swept across Europe and more and more German manpower was drawn to the front, the Czech partisans in our area became bolder. Some of the boys from our school disappeared. Several were later found murdered in the street. Adults cursed us and even little children stuck out their tongues as we marched from the Villa to our dining hall near the train station.

The worst time was at night when we had to stand guard. We formed a sentry line and stood in darkness and total silence around the villa, eyes and ears alert for an intruder. We had no weapons other than our daggers, which, we knew, would be useless against even the smallest gun. We hid our fears as best we could, but we could see in the faces of those around us a mirror of our own qualms.

I remembered then how much I had longed for the

day when I could join the German Youth and how much I looked forward to becoming a full-fledged Hitler Youth at fourteen. I had gone to meetings gladly, taken the tests in athletics, learned map reading and military science. I had studied the biographies of Hitler and our other leaders and wondered if I'd ever rise to such heights.

History was one of my favorite subjects. I resented the shameful Treaty of Versailles that had stripped Germany of her rightful land, and I was proud when we had taken it back, plus more as the war began. Most of all, I loved to sing "*Deutschland, Deutschland, über Alles,*" expressing my conviction that Germany was indeed above every other country.

Then came the Sunday meetings. The Fuehrer saw to it that we had little time for worshipping the Jew Jesus, but my father insisted that my place was in church with him. Not that I minded being in church. But I felt that my duty to the Fatherland, especially during this time of war, meant that I should instead march and train with the other boys on that day.

I knew, of course, that my father also loved his country. He had been born in East Prussia, a German enclave surrounded by Poland and Russia, and, perhaps because of this proximity to other countries, was deeply patriotic. He went into the army, but, since his heart also beat for God, he managed to get free on weekends and come back to pastor his church.

When my father forbade Siegfried and me to miss church more than once a month, we knew it would be trouble. Twice I was asked to take home a note admonishing my parents for my irregular attendance on Sundays. But my father insisted, "Give to Caesar what is Caesar's and to God what is God's. Sunday belongs to God, so you will go to his house."

68

There was no arguing with my father on such matters.

One evening, however, my platoon leader and a youth commander came to our house. I was impressed because a youth commander was the leader of about six hundred German Youth.

But they had not come for a social visit. They came only to impress upon my father the need for his sons to take part in German Youth meetings on Sunday. Nervously I waited for the clash.

"On Sundays my boys go to church," my father told the visitors in warm but certain tones.

"They can go in the evening," the youth commander countered.

"They will be in church in the morning *and* in the evening," my father insisted.

"Twice?" The youth leader furrowed his brow.

"Twice!"

On one side sat the tall, uniformed sergeant major, a military decoration on his lapel. Across from him the German Youth leader was young enough to be his son. The discussion became hotter and the voices louder.

"All right for now," the youth commander finally declared. "We will go, but you haven't heard the last of us."

They clicked their heels, made the proper stiff-arm salute with a snappy "Heil Hitler," and left without a further word.

I watched them leave, speechless, impressed that my father had stood his ground. On the other hand, I wanted to go to the meetings, and I had one last card to play.

"What's wrong with going to the youth film showings?" I asked provocatively.

"Nothing is wrong with the youth films, but why do

they have to be on Sunday? The party is trying to pull you from the old church ways." He answered me matter-of-factly, not expecting the blow I was about to deal him.

"Is it better to stay home on Sunday and listen to the BBC from England?"

My brother gasped and my father's head whirled around.

"I hate it when you come home and listen to the enemy," I shouted, close to tears.

My father knew the danger. It was strictly forbidden to listen to the German-language programs from England, and one could be arrested for doing it. In school we were taught to watch for our parents' disobedience and report them to the authorities. Then they would be "invited" to a special camp for an orientation program to learn the ways of the new Germany.

Instead of arguing or threatening, however, he pulled me over and sat me on his lap. "I love you, my son, and I want the best for you. Trust me. I know what is good for you." And to my feeble protests he added, "Some day you'll be grateful to me that I put God over the Fuehrer."

I noticed that he had not answered my questions, but it felt so good to be surrounded by his strong arms and his love that I looked up at him and whispered, "I love you, too, Daddy."

All this seemed so long ago and Berlin so far away. While I still wanted to be a good German Youth, I would gladly have traded Sunday morning political instruction classes for a seat in church.

One day Kurt called us and put us through our drills and close-order-routine until we had sharpened every turn and step. Then without telling us where we were going, he marched us off to the train station for a weekend trip.

We really didn't care where we were going. It was such a relief to be out of the Villa Fragner and out of yelling distance from Herr Grothe. An hour and a half later we got off the train and joined another group of uniformed boys and a convoy of military vehicles in a large square.

As we stood smartly at attention, a contingent of high-ranking military officers appeared, and a national director of youth mounted a small wooden platform. A youth director was second only to Baldur von Schirach, who was second only to the Fuehrer, who was the closest thing to God in our eyes.

"German youth!" he began, "today is an important day in your lives. While our beloved Fuehrer, Adolf Hitler, is untiringly concerned for the well-being of the whole German empire, he is not too busy to think of you. He knows about his boys and girls in the occupied countries, and he wants you to know that he is proud of you."

He stopped to let the words sink in and to ready himself for the more important part of his speech.

"Surrounded by hostile and warfaring countries, Germany has taken up the challenge of defending everything noble, decent, and good. Germans world-wide unanimously proclaim their loyalty to one man, to our Fuehrer, Adolf Hitler. He has thrown off the yoke of shame from Germany's shoulders. We Germans can look up again in pride and know that we are the true heirs of the fearless Germanic tribes that long ago were victorious over all other tribes.

"The world may laugh at us and say that the Fuehrer is at his wit's end, but I tell you that we are only at the beginning of the glorious path on which Adolf Hitler will lead us. Germany will grow larger and stronger.

71

"It will become more beautiful. The Fuehrer's plans include the reorganization of the whole world. Boys, I envy you for the future you will be privileged to experience."

I was deeply moved. How wonderful it was to belong to a united nation under the leadership of a great man. Yes, he had my undivided love and loyalty. At that moment I was willing to lay down my life for the Fuehrer.

But the youth director was not through. He raised his voice and almost shouted across the square, now filled with about 1,500 eager boys.

"But you will have to fight for it. And for that you will need a strong body and a healthy mind. And you will need one more thing—weapons."

His words were music to my ears. How often had we wished for a rifle or a revolver when the Czechs ambushed our marching formation and bombarded us with stones.

"It is, therefore, my great privilege to pronounce you today to be of the right age to become a Hitler Youth. Our beloved Fuehrer, Adolf Hitler, recognizes how much the war years have matured you, and how you are able to shoulder greater responsibilities."

Just like that. I was only thirteen, but in this special time of need I was pronounced fourteen. What a wonderful new order this was. I was sure nothing like this had ever happened to my parents or grandparents. Only the New Germany could offer such a chance to a young boy! I was suddenly fourteen years old. Fourteen!

"Whenever your name is called, you will step forward and receive the swastika band. I am proud to have been chosen by the Fuehrer to bring you this good news. To our Fuehrer a triple *Sieg Heil! Sieg Heil! Sieg Heil!*"

I don't know whether our leaders had planned it, but it seemed that we almost spontaneously started to sing the national anthem, *"Deutschland, Deutschland, über Alles. . . ."*

"Kerstan."

I stopped dreaming and with a firm step marched toward the military brass and came to a clicking halt. The director of youth shook my hand, and one of the military officers slipped the red armband up my sleeve. My "Thank you" almost got stuck in my throat. A skillful about-face and a few steps brought me back to my formation.

One by one others were called, and I could see the pride and joy in their faces. This was a great occasion that we'd remember all our lives. I glanced at the swastika on my arm, a symbol that someday we would rule the world. And Adolf Hitler's words came to mind. I had memorized them for political instruction tests:

> The swastika flag—what a symbol it is! In RED we see the social ideal of the movement, in WHITE the nationalist ideal, in the SWASTIKA the mission of the struggle for the victory of the Aryan man.

Thank God I was not a Jew, but an Aryan man! Now, at fourteen, a real man.

IX

In spite of what the party decreed, I was really only
thirteen in the spring of 1945. But I had, undoubtedly,
developed some hard edges. I had endured bombings,
months of hard military training, and years of incessant
state propaganda. Now I had a gun and a grenade
thrust into my hands, and I thought I was ready for war.
Barely an hour had passed since our transformation
into manhood before the soldiers took us out to the
target ranges and began our instruction. Underneath
that thin crust, however, I had a soft core of Christian
love that both bewildered me and frustrated me in my
effort to be a good soldier.

I had no trouble firing a rifle at a target. I was a good
shot, and four of my first six bullets hit the bull's-eye.
It was the hand grenade exercise that stopped me.

When my first grenade fell far short of the mark, the

instructor growled at me. "Throw it hard. Think of the target as a Jew. You want to kill a Jew, don't you?"

Suddenly I saw a Jew standing there but it was someone I knew—Dr. Gruenbaum, our family doctor. I had known him as a kind man, gentle, always with a piece of candy for me when I went to his office.

One day I saw *"Jude"* (Jew) printed in big red letters on his door, and his practice was closed. Several days later I saw him coming down the street, sweeping the sidewalks and gutters, a bright yellow star sewed to his shirt.

"Dr. Gruenbaum," I quickly addressed him, stepping up to shake his hand.

For a brief moment he looked up, forced the shadow of a smile on his tired face, and walked slowly away. Further down the street he started sweeping again, burying his head deeply between his shoulders.

I stormed up to our apartment and bombarded my mother with questions. But she didn't know how to explain to a ten-year-old son that there was no room for Jews in Germany, that the government was doing everything to degrade, humiliate, deprive, and eventually eliminate them all.

From then on, almost every afternoon, I watched my "Uncle Doctor" come down the street, swinging the broom as best he could. He looked sick, and he didn't have his usual smile. One day I saved a half slice of my bread, and when Dr. Gruenbaum walked by, I quickly put the slice of bread in his hand and said, "Here, please eat this, Uncle Doctor."

He was so surprised he let the bread slip out of his hand, but I quickly picked it up from the pavement and gave it to him again.

"Watch out, child," the old man said. He put the bread into his pocket and continued sweeping.

"Why did he say 'Watch out'?" I asked my brother.

"Because it is a dumb thing to give bread to a Jew."

"Why is it so dumb?" I persisted.

"You're a member of the Hitler Youth and you don't know that?" my brother asked sarcastically. "You still have a lot to learn, especially not to feed Jews."

That didn't sound like Siegfried. He liked Dr. Gruenbaum, too. But he was older and had more experience in the Hitler Youth; evidently I had missed the instructions concerning the treatment of Jewish family doctors.

Two days later I again pocketed a slice of bread. It was hard, but it felt like a treasure in my hand.

"Uncle Doctor!" I jumped into the street, but stopped abruptly, thinking of his warning words. He had seen my unfortunate maneuver and smiled. I let him come closer to me as he was sweeping, and without a word I dropped the bread into the side pocket of his overcoat. As I pulled out my hand, he grabbed it and held it for a moment. At the same time he looked into my eyes, and I saw how his eyes filled up with tears.

"Thank you, my good boy," he whispered more with his eyes than with his lips.

"Think of the target as a Jew," the Hitler Youth instructor barked, shattering my thoughts. I was doing that, however, and that was what kept me from throwing.

"What's the matter, Kerstan?" He looked at me sharply. "Don't you want to kill a Jew?"

Almost sick with the idea, I tried to push Dr. Gruenbaum out of my mind and hurled the grenade as hard as I could. It fell short of the mark, but the instructor must have put it down to my small size and lack of strength.

The training continued back at the Villa. In the morning we tried to concentrate on Latin, French, mathematics, biology, and chemistry, but we lived for

77

the afternoons of military strategy, target practice, and endurance marches. Somebody in Berlin evidently had plans for us.

The enemy had their plans, too, however. British dive bombers began to make daily runs over the town, flying so low we could see the faces of the pilots. There was no warning. They dropped out of the sky spitting steel, and we learned to throw ourselves to the ground without thinking.

We were marching in formation one day when a bomber shot out from behind a factory building, aiming directly toward us. With not even seconds to move, we looked straight into the guns of the diving plane. Suddenly the plane pulled up, nearly hitting another building but leaving us frozen in fear where we stood.

The drastic change in the life and routine of the Villa had one side benefit. It seemed to keep us out of the range of Herr Grothe's temper, and he had less time to call us out and harangue us.

He was not to be denied completely, however. On a bright Saturday morning in April, Kurt lined us up in formation, and we waited until Herr Grothe came out of the Villa, followed by his wife, who carried a big box. He posted himself in front of us and with a plastic smile began his speech.

"Today our beloved Fuehrer, Adolf Hitler, has prepared a special surprise for you." He touched his party membership pin reverently as he paused. "He has not forgotten your sacrifice and has sent something for you which is very hard to get."

Was it food? A special sweet? More likely some new clothes to replace the well-worn ones we had on our backs. Perhaps even a watch? We waited eagerly.

Herr Grothe opened the box ceremoniously, prolonging his moment of control. Then he produced a toothbrush and toothpaste and held them high.

"See, these are the Fuehrer's favors to you."

I could feel each boy around me hold back the groan within him. What a crummy favor! Meanwhile, Herr Grothe began to pass them out, passing over the brush and paste with one hand and shaking the boys' hands with the other. The thank-yous he received as he worked his way down the line brought an even wider smile to his face.

I looked at the toothpaste in my hand, knowing that it had a terrible taste. It surely wasn't much that the Fuehrer sent from Berlin.

"What did he call this stuff?" I whispered to my neighbor. "A special favor from the Fuehrer? I'll tell you what it is." My voice gained some volume, because I wanted all my classmates to hear my joke.

"This represents the Fuehrer's undying faith that we have not lost our teeth and there is still something left to be brushed."

Some of the boys chuckled, spurring me to continue a little louder.

"Actually, this paste is made of Indian war paint, tennis shoe whitener and, last but not least, toothpaste. Therefore, it is called 'war-paint-shoe-tooth-applicator.'"

Herr Grothe must have heard the last few words, because he suddenly stopped in his activity and asked sharply, "Who said that? I want to know who made those remarks about the toothpaste!"

"I did," I confessed, marveling at my own courage, and regretting it at the same time.

"You! It's you again!" He searched for words.

"Step up here!" he ordered. I took one step forward, while he moved in on me, towering over me.

"Turn around so that everybody can see you! Are you not ashamed of yourself? Our Fuehrer sends us these special favors and you, you good-for-nothing, thank him by insulting him."

With that he handed the box back to his wife to free his hands for a more important purpose. He hit me with his left and then his right, steel-braced hand. He slapped me again and again, while his anger seemed to rise.

"You clergy creep! You idiot! You half Jew! You stupid Baptist!"

He kept hitting me on my cheeks, my ears, my head, and my neck. The more I tried to duck, the harder he hit me. But I didn't cry. Not even a sigh came from my lips. I would not give him that satisfaction.

He stopped abruptly, wiped his hands, tried to catch his breath, and reached for the box again. I stood at attention, but my cheeks burned and I felt something trickling down my ear. Don't weaken now, I told myself, and to overcome the pain and the shame I put on a big grin. Some boys smiled back.

With that, Herr Grothe lost control again. Clutching the box to his chest with his left arm, he hammered at my face with his steel hand. One strike hit me above the eye, so that my eyes began to water.

"There," he yelled triumphantly holding my badly bruised face by the chin and showing it to my classmates.

"There is your hero. Look, and look good! Now he is crying like a baby."

Doomed to remaining passive they just stood there, knowing why my eyes were watering, their own eyes filled with hatred. Herr Grothe must have felt it, because he hurriedly finished his distribution and ordered Kurt to take over. Then he disappeared with Frau Grothe into the Villa.

All Kurt could do was to dismiss us, and the boys crowded around me. The brutal beating made them forget any fear of reprisals for associating with me. One of the boys took his handkerchief and wiped the blood off my ear and my uniform, and Richard put his hand on my shoulder.

"That man is crazy," he spat. "Wait till we get back to Berlin, we'll report him to the police."

"Or we'll kill him first," added Horst.

As I walked up the Villa steps, my legs felt rubbery and my head throbbed. But I knew that one more band had been forged between the platoon and myself. I was one of them now, but more than that. I had suffered for them and I knew they'd remember that.

X

I was right about one thing. I had earned the respect of the boys in that camp. They no longer mocked me for my daily Bible reading and praying, and while they showed no signs of interest in God, they didn't seem to mind if I stayed on good terms with him.

I felt the need of that relationship more and more those days, for something was in the air. A certain nervousness in the teachers, a whisper in the mess hall, a hurried messenger. We didn't know for certain what it was, but we could guess.

Finally the order came—prepare to evacuate. We didn't have much to pack, but Herr Grothe insisted we leave the Villa the way we found it. So we put all our school supplies neatly into boxes, raked leaves, and cleaned the dormitory rooms while we waited. Still, we were surprised when a military courier on motorcycle hurriedly drove up and leaned on the bell outside the gate.

"Let's go, you boys, I don't have all day." Then he broke into a nasty laugh when he saw what we were doing. "Good grief, Germany is being wiped from the map and here you are raking leaves."

When Kurt came to the gate, he opened it and saluted the courier with a stiff "Heil Hitler!" But the man brushed him aside with an "Okay, okay, hail to him," and rushed in to find Herr Grothe.

We stood nailed to the spot, appalled at the brash, unmilitary manner. On his way out he hurled another verbal grenade.

"Throw away those rakes and run for your lives, boys. If the Russians don't catch you, the Americans will."

Then he revved the motor, jerked the machine into gear, and raced away.

It was the first time we'd ever heard such talk. Was he a communist or a deserter? Could he really be a German soldier? He certainly hadn't shaken our faith in the Thousand Year Reich, but perhaps he had forced the first invisible crack that would eventually bring that faith down in ruins around us.

I had no time to speculate, however. We hastily stuffed everything except blankets into our knapsacks and marched to the dining hall. For once we were allowed to eat all we wanted and Herr Grothe produced a bottle of wine. Filling his wife's glass and his own, he toasted, "To Germany! To the shortening of our battle fronts! To the final victory!" It was an empty gesture, and Frau Grothe echoed it weakly.

That night the soldier's remarks ran through my head along with Herr Grothe's toast—"To the shortening of the battle front." We knew very little of what was really happening in the war. The authorities told us that the Allied advance was part of the German strategy to shorten the distance to the fronts. We had heard of the

V-1 and V-2 rockets that bombed England, and we expected that everything was leading up to the V-3. That, we were sure, would end the war. Perhaps that was at hand. And perhaps they'd send us to the front along with other Hitler Youth for that final victory. They certainly had given us no indication of where we were going. With mixed excitement and fear I hoped to be part of the great final struggle.

Herr Grothe woke us at five the next morning and we marched to the station. From then on confusion and indecision reigned. There was no train, nor was there any food. When a train and rations did appear, the British bombers zoomed out of the western sky and strafed the station, blowing up the locomotive. Hours later, when another locomotive puffed into the station to replace it, a single British plane dropped down and planted a bomb directly in the boiler. Finally the High Command send a third locomotive and we quickly boarded, anxious to get out of that place. Hours passed. We slept. When we awoke, we found the train hadn't moved an inch. It was an ominous start.

"Wheels must roll for victory," some wag remarked. It was one of the endless slogans we'd learned to accept as part of life.

"Yeah, but where?" Juergen voiced the question we all held back.

Hungry—we'd only eaten once the day before—we tried to keep up a brave front as we huddled on the wooden coach benches. Two of our group, Walter and Erwin, had been killed in the strafing, but we said little about it. "Don't weaken! Close your eyes to pity," we'd been taught.

But I didn't feel strong. Loneliness, pity, fear, and hopelessness lurked just below the surface. I managed to push them down once again.

We had boarded a refugee train with hundreds of other Hitler Youth, both boys and girls. Somehow or other our old dormitory gang managed to stay together. After several false starts and partisan attacks, the train slipped out of Rewnitz late at night and headed southeast. We had no idea where we were going and had been severely reprimanded for using the term "fleeing."

After hours of traveling, Herr Grothe announced that we were heading for Schwarz-Indien, but none of us had ever heard of that. We never, in fact, got to Schwarz-Indien but instead crisscrossed the country from the Austrian border to Poland and west toward Germany, back and forth, stopping only for fuel or when we were attacked by dive bombers or partisans.

When the train slowed down, we readied ourselves for the cry "Jump out and take cover." Man, that was fun!—to jump from a moving train and hear the ack-ack-ack of the antiaircraft gun on top of our car.

"Russian planes," Werner commented as we dove one time.

"No, they're British," Juergen argued.

It was the type of discussion we might have had playing our war games a year or so before. They were Russian planes, however, and we knew what that meant. The British had strafed the train briefly and gone after the locomotive to stop it. The Russians, however, made a deadly game out of their attacks. This time they came back again and again, in spite of the Red Cross markings on the top of the train.

When the attack was over, Herr Grothe blew his whistle and yelled for us to hurry back.

"Come on," I shouted to the boy beside me. "They won't wait for us."

He didn't move and I called again. "Let's go, what's your name anyhow?"

As I bent down to grab his arm, I saw the blood on his face and knew instantly that he was dead.

"Reinhold," my friends and Herr Grothe were yelling desperately.

"I can't come. This boy's been hit."

"Is he dead?"

"Yes, he's dead."

"Then get back here, you stupid boy," Herr Grothe snarled.

"Can't we bury him?"

"Reinhold, I'll give you ten seconds and then this train is moving." He began to count, and, gritting my teeth, I jerked myself away from the dead boy and ran.

"That's a boy," Herr Grothe said approvingly, and I suppose I should have been pleased that for once he had said something good about me. In that moment, however, I resented him. I hated the cold efficiency that denied a feeling of the heart. I hated him also because he had removed the party membership pin that he always wore in his lapel. Was our German ship of state really sinking and this rat jumping ship? The train began to roll, and I huddled against the wall, fearing to hear the cry to take cover again.

It wasn't long in coming. Again we dove into the dirt and grass beside the tracks. As I pressed my face into the mud, I heard the drone of motors overhead.

Herr Grothe yelled, "Attacking planes!"

Horst, who shared the same small depression in the ground with me, yelled back in jest, "Good observation," and raised his head to see where Herr Grothe's voice came from. As he did, I heard the whine of bullets coming toward us, and Horst's face exploded, blood and flesh flying into my own face. Then I heard others cry out in pain as the bullets cut a path across the field of boys. For a long time I laid still, not wanting to ever look up again, the image of Horst's face forcing itself on my mind.

Finally a hand shook my shoulder, "Hey, little fellow. You okay?" I turned reluctantly to look at a German soldier standing above me. He had thrown a jacket over Horst, and I reached over to remove it and see if it was all true.

"Don't," he commanded. "He's dead. Finished. You can't help him."

He offered me water from his canteen, but I knew I couldn't hold it down. A Red Cross train had come up behind us and set up a field hospital tent. Werner and Richard and some of the others were taking provisions the soldiers shared, and I walked over to them.

"Wipe the blood off your face." Werner's voice was hard.

"Why haven't you poor kids gone home?" the soldiers asked us.

I drew myself up to my full five feet and answered him proudly. "Because the Fuehrer doesn't want us home. First we have to win the final victory."

The soldier who had helped me dealt the blow swiftly. "Don't you realize Germany has lost the war? Russian tanks are a few miles to the east and the Americans are only a few miles to the west. It's all over. Only Berlin is holding out."

I had the feeling I shouldn't listen to that kind of talk, that I should block my ears and run.

Instead I stood there staring, resenting the pity they showed for what they called our "blind faith." I heard what he said, but I couldn't understand.

Without warning I felt the world begin to shake and crumble. Lose the war? Why hadn't we ever had a chance to fight? Here was a train full of able Hitler youth aching to get into the struggle. Had we been lied to, deceived? My mind refused to accept it. The seed had been planted and was taking root too quickly. Numbly I accepted the chocolate and cheese the soldiers offered, shook hands, and followed the other boys back to the train.

XI

I had always been able to talk to my father. If I interrupted him in his study, he'd set aside his Bible or sermon preparation, and we'd have a conversation about whatever was on my mind. Often in recent months, I longed to talk to him and cried to myself, "Father, are you there? I need your counsel."

Now I badly felt the need of his wisdom. Something was terribly wrong, and, as much as I had faith in the Fuehrer and the leaders of the Third Reich, I trusted one person even more—my father. However, I had no idea where he was. The last letter I received said he had been transferred to Italy. I knew my mother had gone back to Berlin.

Late one night, after almost a week of erratic chasing back and forth across Czechoslovakia, we were transferred to open freight cars with more boys from other schools, and finally crossed into Austria. There we zig-zagged again along a narrow corridor, trying to avoid the Allied forces closing in from both sides. Our leaders still had the idea that we should get back to Berlin to help the Fuehrer in his last stand, but we had gone nearly two days without food, making little progress toward Germany.

On the third morning, before the others were awake, I lay on my belly in the straw and reached for my Bible, but I brushed Richard as I did so and awakened him. He looked at me sadly, and on impulse I asked him, "Do you want me to read out loud?"

"Yeah, yeah! Just don't read too loud and wake up the others."

I turned to a psalm that I had found comforting before and began to whisper:

> Hear my prayer, O Lord;
> give ear to my supplications!
> In thy faithfulness answer me,
> in thy righteousness!
> Enter not into judgment with thy servant;
> for no man living is righteous before thee.
> For the enemy has pursued me;
> he has crushed my life to the ground;
> he has made me sit in darkness like those long dead.
> Therefore my spirit faints within me;
> my heart within me is appalled.
> I remember the days of old,
> I meditate on all that thou hast done;
> I muse on what thy hands have wrought.
> I stretch out my hands to thee;
> my soul thirsts for thee like a parched land.
> Make haste to answer me, O Lord!
> My spirit fails!
> Hide not thy face from me, lest I be like those who go
> down to the Pit.

Let me hear in the morning of thy steadfast love,
for in thee I put my trust.
Teach me the way I should go,
for to thee I lift up my soul.
Deliver me, O Lord, from my enemies!
I have fled to thee for refuge!
Teach me to do thy will,
for thou art my God!
Let thy good spirit lead me
on a level path!
For thy name's sake, O Lord, preserve my life!
In thy righteousness bring me out of trouble!
And in thy steadfast love cut off my enemies,
and destroy all my adversaries, for I am thy servant.

When I finished reading, Richard was quiet for a long time. Then he commented:

"Wow, that's powerful. Who said that, Jesus?"

"No, King David of Israel. He was a wise king and one of the direct forefathers of Jesus."

"Does it really say there that God should cut off my enemies and destroy them?"

"That's what it says. But I like most the part where he prays, 'Let me hear in the morning of thy steadfast love, for in thee I put my trust. Teach me the way I should go, for to thee I lift up my soul.' "

"Right!" Richard whispered. "Are you going to pray now?" he then asked.

"Yep, that's what I usually do after I read the Bible."

Richard was quiet again.

"You want me to pray out loud?"

"That's all right. Just pray for yourself. I think the others are waking up now. But listen, Reinhold, make sure you include me in your prayers."

"I will," I replied, choking on the lump in my throat.

That night the locomotive pulled us up into the Hohe Tauern Mountains and stopped. The doors of our freight car had been nailed open and the cold wind blew straight in so that we lay shivering for hours. Dysentery had spread through the group, and through the long night one boy after the other rose silently, disappeared out the door, then some time later weakly climbed back in. Some of the boys complained about cramps or pain in their lungs.

Tim, a slightly built blond boy from Potsdam, had a fever so high it didn't seem he could live much longer.

"He needs broth, tea, and soft-cooked eggs to help him get well," one of the soldiers told us, but the advice was so ridiculous in that situation that we just laughed. For the past two days our food had been little more than grass and water.

I think everyone else was asleep and it was still dark when I noticed Tim get up, walk to the open door and stand there for a moment. Then he was gone. I thought he must have fallen, but I didn't hear anything and dozed off again.

It was beginning to get light when a voice woke us, "Where's Tim?"

We roused and looked around.

"Where is he?" It was one of the leaders, yelling now.

"He walked out to ease himself," I answered.

"What do you mean he walked out? He didn't even have the strength to get up. Did you see him?"

"Yessir."

"Then come and look for him," he screamed at me.

The terrain near the tracks was treacherous—big boulders, gullies, patches of snow, slippery ground. I wanted to find Tim because I had seen him leave. I knew he was sick, but I'd done nothing to help him, not even call for someone else.

I worked my way over the rough ground as quickly as my own strength would let me, but someone else found him first.

"Over here," a voice called.

Tim's body was draped across a rock about fifteen feet down in a small gorge. His feet had caught in the branch of a pine and his head dangled down. It was obvious that he was dead.

I couldn't take my eyes off the grisly scene. The question rang over and over in my mind, "Why didn't you help him?" Had my own comfort meant more to me? In Sunday school we had learned we were to love our neighbors as ourselves, and I knew Tim was my neighbor.

It was still morning when the train stopped in Schladming. Juergen and I slipped off the side of the freight car and wandered through the train yard in search of scraps, anything edible. A military train had pulled into the station, and we caught the strong smell of soup coming from steaming kettles. Our train might pull away if we stayed to investigate, but, I agreed with Juergen, they'd probably never miss us.

As we'd hoped, the soldiers knew what we wanted.

"Look at those little animals," they said with both amazement and affection.

"Dirty little rascals."

"I'll bet they're hungry."

We had strong feelings for the soldiers. They were our heroes, and here was a group that had obviously seen action. They shoved messtins in our hands and made us sit down and eat, but we didn't know when to stop. Our shriveled stomachs rebelled, and the soldiers watched in pity as we lost all that we had greedily gulped down. No one laughed, but I felt unclean both inside and out. My uniform was streaked with blood and vomit. My black shorts had holes in them and hadn't been washed for weeks.

A gray-haired captain who appeared to be the officer in charge began to question us.

"Why don't you ride the train through the American lines?" he asked gently, somehow combining the manner of a stern military veteran with that of a kindly grandfather.

I looked up in surprise. "They'd kill us, of course."

"Nonsense! No soldier would kill you youngsters," he scoffed.

"Oh, yes, they would." I hastened to assure him. "We've read stories and seen movies. They'll murder us."

"Aw, that's just propaganda. Do you believe those stories? Look at yourself. Do you look like a super race? You're close to starvation."

I noticed that while he was talking an S.S. trooper in black uniform had walked up behind him and stood quietly listening. I was glad he was there, because I was afraid the old soldier would manage to turn us against the Germany we believed in. The S.S. man, I knew, would help to keep us straight.

"The Czechs killed a lot of us Hitler youth," Juergen kept on.

"That's different. You were in enemy territory. They were trying to get back at Germany and took it out on you. But the Americans won't harm you."

Some of the soldiers tried to signal the officer secretly that the S.S. man was behind him. "Why should we run to the enemy now when Hitler is ready to launch the V-3? Then we'll reconquer all our lost territory and all Europe as well."

The officer burst into laughter. "You can't be serious.

You really believe those stories about a miracle weapon?"

He still hadn't seen the S.S. man and continued. "That Adolf is a master faker. Even now when everything is lost, you still believe in him. Don't you realize that. . . ."

"That's enough!" snapped the trooper, stepping in front of him. "Hand me your pistol," he ordered, stretching out his arm.

"Take your dirty hands off me," the army officer snarled. "Who gives you the right to censure me?"

"I do, in the Fuehrer's name. You've promoted anti-German thoughts; you've called the Fuehrer a master faker; you told these boys that Germany has lost the war. Now give me your weapon and follow me to the Military Tribunal."

But the old captain would have none of it. "How dare you insult me! I served in World War I when you were still a baby. And I've seen action in Russia, Africa and France in this war. And where have you been, you Blackshirt? Look here. . . ." He wrestled a knight's cross, a high German decoration from underneath the scarf he had around his neck. "Do you think the Army hands these out to cowards?"

But the S.S. man was unmoved. He looked the officer coldly in the eyes and said,

"I give you ten seconds to make up your mind and follow me. If you don't obey, I'll shoot you down as a deserter. You know Hitler's order, 'Death for any soldier who retreats.' "

"Who retreats here?" one of the soldiers asked angrily.

"This officer does," the black-uniformed trooper answered. "You heard what he said. He's already in full retreat."

That was too much for the aged officer's honor. He took a quick step toward his accuser as though to hit him. Like lightning, however, the S.S. man reached for his revolver and fired into the belly of the officer.

I wanted to scream and run, but neither my legs nor my voice would obey me. I sat numbly, only faintly hearing the second and third shots. The officer tried to speak, but nothing came from his lips. He pressed both hands against his belly, started to sway, then suddenly dropped to the ground.

The trooper looked at the barrel of his pistol, blew the smoke off as though he were in a cowboy movie, and calmly put it back into his holster. No one moved nor said a word. The wounded man had fallen against our feet, but we didn't dare reach for him.

"Heil Hitler!" The Blackshirt saluted, clicked his heels, and marched away.

Then something in me snapped. I jumped up and Juergen followed. We dashed toward our own train, bumping blindly into soldiers and baggage, tripping on tracks and railroad ties until we found our freight car and pulled ourselves in. Juergen lay there with his hands covering his head, and I fell onto the straw, my head spinning, aware but hardly caring that a car full of boys was staring at us.

The shots that killed the soldier had shattered something in me. This couldn't be the Germany I had imagined. What had happened to the goodness, the justice, the rightness of the super race? Had I made that up? In the eyes of that officer, I had seen a small flame of human kindness, but the S.S. man had snuffed it out in the Fuehrer's name.

In that cruel moment of realism I had seen a cutaway view of the Third Reich, and all my Christian training and reading of the Word of God told me it was wrong.

There was more to life than that, more than just political propaganda, marching to orders, shooting, and eating. There was something deeper in us—a common humanity—and I had seen that denied.

Guilt swept over me. I had been a part of it and perhaps the guiltiest of all because I knew better. I had heard the gospel of love. I had seen it and felt it. Yet I had hardened my heart and put my pride in the super race before my love of God.

I wrapped my arms around me, unable to cry, futilely trying to shut out the terrifying scene. As the train began to roll, the hard clack of the wheels echoed again and again in the emptiness of my soul.

The tears I couldn't weep that morning were only hours away, however. The next time our train stopped, we found more soldiers, and these appeared to be drunk. They were bawling out a tune they had made up themselves:

Der Papst ist tot.
Der Papst ist tot.
Die Katholiken sind in Not.

(The Pope is dead; the Pope is dead. The Catholics are in a fix.)

We couldn't figure out why the Pope's death would cause them to celebrate, so we asked them.

"Are you kids Catholic?" they wanted to know.

"No!" Wolfgang told them. "We're *Gottgläubige.*" That was a term the Nazis had invented and literally meant "believers in God." But it referred to the gods of Germanic origin, not to the God of the Bible. The *Gottglaeubigen* believed in the state and the mystical religion of a super race.

"Then what do you care if the Pope is dead?"

"Well, is he?" we pressed them.

"Well, no! Not really. *He's* not the one who's dead."

We were just about to dismiss this whole thing as the stupid antics of drunk soldiers when one of them blurted out: "It's your pope who's dead. Your big leader. The Fuehrer."

Very slowly the words sank into my consciousness. What had he said? The Fuehrer dead? A lie! A big lie! The Fuehrer couldn't die. That could happen to other human beings, but not to the Fuehrer!

When they saw the surprise and doubt on our faces, they sobered up.

"Didn't you know? Hadn't you heard?" they all shouted.

No, we didn't know and we hadn't heard, and now we couldn't believe it. Over the past few weeks we'd learned that soldiers are good natured, often willing to share their food rations with us and care for us. But you couldn't trust the words of adults. They looked on Hitler Youth as kids, and they liked to scare us with stories of approaching armies and of losing the war. Was this just another prank?

Gradually I realized that every word they said was true. They told of Hitler's death with so much conviction I knew they weren't teasing. As we pieced together the story, we learned that just a few hours ago the German radio had announced that Hitler had died defending Berlin against the Russians. Grand Admiral Karl Doenitz was his successor.

"At least that's what we heard on the radio," one of the soldiers said apologetically.

Then they began discussing Adolf Hitler in a way I'd never heard before in my life, and I was shocked.

"They say he died fighting, but I don't believe it."

"He never fired a shot."

"Probably flew off to Switzerland."

100

One young soldier rallied to the Fuehrer's defense. "In my book he's still the greatest hero of the German Reich," he said.

"Well, you'd better burn that book," an older veteran warned him, "because they'll have some other names for him in the future."

The voices faded—or perhaps I just stopped listening. Adolf Hitler, my beloved Fuehrer, had died. Crushed with grief, I crawled back into a corner of the freight car and started to weep. Yes, I cried, great wracking sobs that had built up in me for years. The old admonition, "A Hitler Youth never cries," meant nothing to me now that he was gone. I was no longer a Hitler Youth. It was over, the dream, the fantasy. No one could ever take his place. The tears, unstoppable, poured down my face.

XII

While our train was scurrying around Austria, Adolf Hitler, in his bunker in Berlin, had picked up a revolver and shot himself in the mouth. Mussolini had been captured several days before by Italian partisans and executed. German troops in Italy had laid down their arms the next day.

The final blow came when we learned that Berlin had surrendered.

Two days later, however, we were still wandering from station to station. Things had actually begun to look a little brighter. Whenever our leaders stopped the train, there was a military station close by, and we usually ended up in a food line at an army canteen. After almost a week of no food, we were now getting one meal a day.

On the night of May 3 while the train was rolling

through a small valley, one of the sick boys walked to the open door and fell to his death. It was senseless to go back and look for his body, and I found myself thinking again, another one who died for folk and Fatherland. Horst, Tim, the old German officer, now this boy. Would we all die, slowly but surely?

The clacking wheels stopped abruptly, interrupting my daydreaming. We weren't at a station, and the train hadn't stopped so quickly since the days when the divebombers were after us. We leaned out and peered as far as we could into the darkness, and then we knew. We were confronted by enemy troops. Our long flight had come to a dishonorable end.

We were in the vicinity of St. Johann im Pongau, some fifty kilometers south of Salzburg, and our train was shunted into a siding. Close to us were prisoner-of-war camps with both Russian and British prisoners, and the American army had just pushed into the area to set them free.

When the Nazis had annexed Austria in 1938, they had changed the name to Ostmark. As soon as they were liberated, the joyful Austrians took swastika flags, removed the black emblem and the white background, and sewed a strip of white cloth across the red, making an Austrian flag.

At the same time, they unleashed a fury of hatred against anything German. When the citizens of St. Johann learned that a stranded trainload of Hitler Youth sat on the outskirts of their town, they came by the hundreds. With sticks, stones, obscenities, and any other weapons they could find, the angry townspeople marched on us bent on revenge.

We heard the shouting, "Kill those Nazis . . . kill them," and looked out to find them crowding the embankment.

"Reinhold!" Herr Grothe's voice pierced my fear. "Reinhold, run! Run for the Americans," he screamed. "Get military protection." I don't know why he picked me for this errand, but he did.

Because I wanted to get out of there, and since I'd been taught to obey without question, I jumped out beside the startled Austrians and began running, not even sure what direction to take. By the time the Austrians realized that only one boy and not a carload was coming out, I was out of range.

I began to pray as I ran, but before I had a chance to get very far, a jeep with two Americans came within inches of running right into me. It took me a few minutes to convey the problem to them, but then they moved quickly. While we sped back toward the train, they notified their commander of the problem.

It was when we got back to the train, however, that I saw the most unlikely scene. The Austrian mob stood some thirty or forty yards from the train, waving rifles, pitchforks and sticks, and shouting. Between them and the train stood about fifty ex-prisoners of war, Russians and British, who had no arms but were intent on saving the lives of the Germans.

Something didn't fit. The Americans and the Russians and the British were our enemies. The Russians will shoot you on sight, I'd been told. The British will take your money and run. The French are worse. And the Americans have thrown in with a bad lot. Here, however, these "enemies" were risking their lives to save ours. I watched, confused and troubled, as American reinforcements came and dispersed the Austrian mob. Again the reality of the moment rubbed against what I had thought to be true. The conviction was slowly building in me that I had been led far astray.

There was still much healing to be done. Sores of

resentment festered far beneath the surface of my consciousness and broke out at unexpected times.

There was still Herr Grothe, for example. If Hitler's death and the collapse of the Third Reich had hit him hard, it certainly hadn't affected his ego. For roll call he made us line up just as he had done every day for the last year. Almost out of habit we obeyed. But then it dawned on us one morning that there was no longer any reason for it.

"I said *Achtung*," he raged one afternoon when we slouched in formation. We pretended we hadn't heard him and he stalked over to where I stood.

"Are you the devil who is starting a revolt again?" he asked without mentioning my name.

I started to burn inside, then quickly decided I'd had enough of that. In mock surprise I looked around.

"Who are you talking to, Herr Grothe?"

"I'm talking to you, you swine," and he shook his fist in front of my face.

It took some effort but I stayed calm. "I have a name, in case you don't remember. It's Reinhold, but you've ignored me so long you've probably forgotten it."

One strong hand grabbed my shoulder and the other swung back but stopped when I said sharply, "I wouldn't do that." It was shock that stopped him, I'm sure, that one of his boys would actually talk that way.

Richard then appeared behind the teacher and pushed his arm down. "You wouldn't want to get hurt as you hurt us, would you?" he mocked.

Grothe was speechless at this disrespect and soon other boys joined in.

"Charges . . . ," he finally said.

But Richard was in no mood for a speech. "Enough of your 'charges,' " he ordered. "We're not your charges anymore."

106

It all happened quickly, spontaneously, and as I watched the school teacher clench his fists and walk away muttering, I remembered that I had pledged eternal revenge on this man. He had beaten me, humiliated me, and made my life miserable for nearly a year. So wasn't I justified in what I said? Perhaps, but I had an uneasy feeling about it. I knew too well what the Bible said about revenge. As hard and cruel as the man had been, he was still another human being.

So several hours later I found myself standing in front of the coach car in which the teachers were living.

"Honey!" I heard Frau Grothe's shrill voice call her husband. "Is that that Reinhold boy out there?"

When Herr Grothe opened the door, he simply stood there and looked at me without speaking.

"Herr Grothe, I came to apologize for my behavior today."

He continued staring at me blankly and I forced myself to go on. "I didn't intend to be insolent. I had just decided I would take no more beatings."

Without a word he stepped down and put his arm around me. He tried to speak but his voice broke. "You poor, poor youngsters." He tried to hide his tears from me and led me away from the train. "Do you know how hard it is to be the leader of a group of boys, first surrounded by partisans, then attacked by bombers. . . ." He went on and on and I had to walk with him and listen. When we arrived back at his coach he thanked me for coming.

"Oh, by the way," he said, "the radio said today that we are living in a democracy. That means the people rule, so there will be no more beatings. Good luck to the people. It was easier with the Fuehrer. He ordered; we followed. I hate to think what it will be like when everybody does just what he wants to do. *Auf wiedersehen!*"

I walked slowly back to my car knowing that the resentment was gone. The visit had released something in me. I knew that Jesus Christ had loved him through me, had done something in me that I could never have done myself, and now I was free from hating Herr Grothe. Now it wouldn't be so hard to pray for him, and, perhaps, one day even to love him.

We sat on that siding outside St. Johann for weeks. Although we began to get food, no one knew what to do with us, and we roamed through the prison camps near the station, getting to know the Russian, British, and American soldiers. Most of us had had four years of English and could get along pretty well at it. When we weren't in the camps, we played games, slipping back into a kind of childhood that had been denied us. We found steel helmets and live grenades, and, with the help of some older boys, soon became demolition experts.

All except Frederick. Frederick had two left hands, and we should have watched him. One day as we carefully opened shells and grenades to get the powder inside, we heard an explosion. Fred slumped and rolled over on the ground, his hand badly burned.

Frederick's injury, however, was overshadowed by another event. Ron, one of the boys in our car, died of cholera. The Austrians wouldn't let him be buried in the town cemetery, so we dug a grave near the train and had an informal funeral service.

One of the Nazi party leaders spoke a few words about Ron dying for the Fatherland. Then suddenly he said, "Let us pray." It must have been spontaneous, something he knew you should do at a funeral, but once he had said it, he didn't know what to do. I could see him looking around for some way out of his dilemma.

Then I saw Herr Grothe trying to catch my eye. He nodded at me, and, not knowing what he wanted, I nodded back. Then I heard him say, "Reinhold will say a prayer for Ronald."

I hesitated, embarrassed, but the party leader followed Herr Grothe's suggestion. "Come, Reinhold, say a prayer for Ronald."

I don't know what they expected, but I stepped forward and closed my eyes. Then I began to talk to God just as I might have done in my own private prayer time. I prayed for the boys who were still sick and I prayed for all of us still living.

No one mocked me, when, a few minutes later, I ran with our gang to the dugout where we had hidden the gunpowder. Only minutes after acting the part of a mature, adult Christian, I was playing boyish games. But the explosives were real.

XIII

At thirteen I had learned the fine art of begging. But the British and Russian POW camps that had been our source of food for several weeks were dissolved, and only a few prisoners were left to care for shutting them down. We stuck close to them, counting on their generosity.

Captain Gregg Davis, a tall, young British officer, had paid special attention to me. He worked on my English pronunciation, and, realizing we had no school, made me translate long articles from the newspaper. In turn I tried to please him, not just for the food he provided but because he was a human who cared about what might happen to me.

One afternoon while I was searching the hills for berries, Gregg Davis appeared, and we began to talk about the future. No one could give us any idea when we might be allowed to return to Berlin, and he knew that I had not heard from my parents for a long time.

"What if you find that your parents have died in the war, Reinhold?"

He asked it kindly and I understood what he meant. It was very possible that I might never see them again, but I avoided thinking of it. Now I just shrugged.

"Would you come to England with me?" He put his arm around my shoulder.

"You think you would want me?" I asked in return.

"Of course . . . look, here's my address." He fished in his pocket for a pencil and paper. "If you should find out sometime that you have no home to go to, I want you to write to me. I'll see to it that you get to England, and my wife and I will take the place of your parents."

Sitting on that hillside and looking down in the valley at our war torn train, I couldn't imagine what it would be like to have a home again. I couldn't hold back the tears, but Captain Davis pretended he didn't see them. We sat for a long time without talking until, reluctantly, we both rose to go back down to the valley.

The next morning Herr Grothe called me to his coach car and I wondered what I had done. To my surprise he offered me a chair. Even Frau Grothe smiled at me.

"Reinhold," he began, trying to adopt a new, friendly manner. "I have given much thought to how to keep our camp alive. We can't just sit here until cholera gets us all. We have to have food—even if we have to steal it."

"But I wouldn't steal it," I interjected.

"I know, I know," he quickly agreed. "That's why I called you. I need some honest boys. I want you to choose three of your friends and form a Food Search Commando unit and go out and find food."

That was how Richard, Juergen, Werner and I happened to start toward town the next morning with a purse crammed full of German marks. I didn't feel that honest, but I had seen boys die of starvation, and I would do anything I could to keep the rest of us from that horror.

Our first attempt was a disaster. We marched boldly into town and down the narrow, cobblestone streets, appealing to the goodheartedness of the shopkeepers. But no one had anything to sell, much less give, to Germans.

As we walked, a second floor window flew open and a woman stuck her head out and yelled: "The nerve of you brown-shirted Nazis coming back to haunt us!"

Werner couldn't resist the taunt and threw back at her, "You know who started it all? The *Austrian*, Adolf Hitler, your native son." That made us feel better but it didn't help us get any food.

After we had tried every bakery and grocery store in town with no success, we finally realized it was our uniforms. The sight of the brown shirts and black pants was too strong a reminder for the Austrians. We had long ago ripped off all the buttons and decorations and exchanged them with the POWs for food, but the image of goose-stepping Nazis with polished brass and leather straps died hard.

"We need civilian clothes, and I know where we can get them," I told my troop, and we headed for the British camp.

Captain Davis was still there, and he rounded up an armload of shirts and pants and jackets. Some of them were big enough for two farmers, but we searched until we had the best fit, laughing at each other and knowing that we looked just as ridiculous ourselves.

Then Gregg Davis suggested, "Let's burn your uniforms."

It seemed like an innocent suggestion to me, although

I wasn't sure how Herr Grothe would take it. Before we could say much, however, the captain had piled the dirty rags outside his tent and poured a bag of gun powder on them.

As I watched the fire consume them, I understood what he had in mind. I thought back to the first day I had worn those clothes and the pride that burst in me as I walked the streets. I had loved that victory rune on the arm band, and I had treasured the swastika. Each symbol had a special meaning, part of the vision of a glorious future, of conquering the entire world.

With glazed eyes I watched that dream go up in the smoke of tattered black shorts and filthy brown shirts. I knew that an important part of my life was going up with it, and I felt cheated, betrayed, used. I had loved Adolf Hitler almost as much as my own father, but now I began to believe what others had said—he was a trickster, a liar, a charlatan. I had defended him before the soldiers who mocked our faith, but they had known better. The image of Hitler as a hero smouldered in the ashes in front of me.

There was so little left of the past, but there was the warm hand on my shoulder and the promise: *My wife and I will take the place of your parents. We'll adopt you.* Yes, and I still had the One whom I had neglected but who would always love me.

In my youthful imagination, the dancing flames took the form of a burnt offering, like the one on the altar of Abel. But I would make sure that no Cain would slay me.

We trudged back to the train, proud of our new clothes, but aware that we returned empty-handed. We quickly drew a crowd of curious boys, and that brought Herr Grothe on the run.

"What's going on here? Reinhold, where is the food?"

"Well, sir, we tried very hard but. . . ." Then I explained that with civilian clothes and the Austrian-German accent I'd practiced, I was sure we could pass as Austrian boys instead of hated Germans. Herr Grothe wasn't entirely convinced, but he had little choice except to let us go the next day.

The first farmer's wife we met wasn't convinced either. "You're those German kids from the train. Get out of here. We don't have enough food for our own kids." It was the same at the next place and the next. The coverup fooled no one.

Hungry, dejected, and afraid to return to camp, we sat on the grass by the road. I looked at the leather purse with more money than I'd ever owned myself and realized how useless it was. If money couldn't buy food, what could? I knew the only answer but was afraid to say it out loud.

"I think we need a different approach," I began hesitatingly.

"You don't say?" mocked Werner.

Juergen and Richard knew me better, however, and looked up expectantly.

"I think we need to pray before we go to the next house," I blurted out.

That's not what Richard and Juergen expected. They looked disgusted.

"So all these farmers are praying, too." Werner pointed out. "Look at all the shrines along the road. Every time they pass one they stop and kneel down."

"I know, I know, but I believe in prayer. Why don't we at least give it a try. What have you got to lose," I added and shrugged.

So at my suggestion we stood in a circle by the side of the road and bowed our heads. "Dear Lord," I spoke out loud, "you know how hungry we are and you know about the boys who are sick. Will you please work in the heart of the farmer there on the hill so that he'll give us food?" It was simple, no frills, but with a new boldness we walked up to the next door and knocked.

"I saw you down there, you boys. What were you doing standing around in a circle? What were you watching?" He sounded suspicious.

Werner couldn't help but laugh as he told him, "We were praying." We expected the farmer to laugh as well, but instead he beckoned us to follow him and led us to a storeroom. There he began scooping flour, sugar, and oats into a few small bags.

"It's all I can give you now." He was apologetic.

"How much do I owe you?"

He thought for a moment. "I'd charge anyone else thirty marks, but I suppose you fellows prayed for a miracle. Well, thirty marks wouldn't look like much of a miracle, so I'll take fifteen."

I didn't argue. I pulled fifteen paper notes from the purse and thanked him. Then we grabbed the bags and quickly walked away.

The farmer at the next place hadn't seen us pray, but apparently God had spoken to him, too. He sold us grain and potatoes, and we headed back to camp with our arms full.

No one mentioned anything about prayer to Herr Grothe. Werner and Richard and Juergen didn't know what to make of it, but I did. It was just one more lesson I had to learn. The faith that I had so easily accepted in the safety and comfort of my father's house was not mine by birth. I had to exercise it, make it mine, use it. I curled up in the freight car that night almost oblivious of my surroundings and almost forgetting that I was still a long way from home—if, that is, I still had one. Something was happening in my life, but I knew that I still had a lot to learn.

The next morning we got up early to build a cart. We had found an old bicycle on the embankment, and we took it apart, saving every bolt and washer. It took us most of the morning, with Herr Grothe hovering over us impatiently, but finally we had something more than our arms in which to carry food for ninety boys.

"Aren't we going to pray first?" Richard queried as we started.

I glanced at Herr Grothe who apparently hadn't understood. "Come, Reinhold," he pushed us along. "The boys are hungry."

Richard was insistent, however. "You have to pray first, Reini. That works better."

So I said a quick prayer without looking at Herr Grothe, grabbed the handle of the cart, and started off.

"Did you see Herr Grothe's face?" Richard laughed. "I'll bet he renames us the Heavenly Food Search Commandoes."

XIV

I don't think anyone who didn't witness Europe in 1945 will ever fully grasp the meaning of the term "displaced persons." The end of hostilities left millions of soldiers and civilians across the continent uprooted. Many, such as our troop of schoolboys, had been evacuated from danger zones. Some had fled advancing armies—probably close to a hundred thousand out of Berlin alone. Others had been deported as slave labor or shipped to prison camps against their will.

Soldiers who laid down their arms were herded into makeshift camps. Civilian camps opened their gates and poured out their prisoners. Hundreds of thousands took off across the countryside to get home the best way they could, but many more thousands had no home to return to.

When the occupation governments hastily took

charge, they had scores of problems. Refugees were only one. In large cities such as Berlin, the military authorities struggled to prevent mass starvation, hold down disease, bury the dead, assure the safety of the population from collapsing ruins, stop looting.

To complicate the refugee problem, the once punctual and smoothly running European railroad system had been devastated. So had the mails. As a crowning blow, the conquering powers—England, the United States, France, and Russia—could not agree among themselves on even the broad principles of occupation, much less the day-by-day details.

Europe's displaced population found itself neglected, unwanted, and often unable or not allowed to go home.

No one gave us any real explanation why we couldn't go back to Berlin, nor did we have any idea of what might await us if we were to get there. A month after our train had been stopped in St. Johann, I still hadn't heard if my parents and brother were alive, and Captain Davis had finally returned to England. Our Food Search Commandoes were meeting with moderate success, but we were still hungry. Herr Grothe nagged us each day to get more food. And we were still living in railroad cars designed for cattle. When the American commander of the area decided to move us into nearby barns, we felt the quality of our lives was definitely improving.

The hay was fresh and we had all the space we needed—at least a square yard or more per person. We carefully laid out our blankets and packs and buried our treasures—bits of chewing gum or chocolate or matches we got from the soldiers—in the hay beneath.

The old gang from our room in the Villa Fragner had managed to stay together. Richard, Juergen, Werner,—even Wolfgang, the bedwetter and bully

—had become part of the group. Shortly after we ran into the Allied forces, we discovered that Wolfgang was a thief. For months back in Rewnitz he had stolen little items—pencils, knives, candy, etc.—from other boys. So we put him under a ban and for weeks didn't speak to him. That ended, however, when we learned that he knew something about explosives and we needed him to help us open live shells without getting blown up.

Wolfgang took the space next to mine when we moved into the barn. I wasn't too pleased about that because I still remembered the cruel hazing he'd initiated at the Villa. But things had changed drastically. My standing with the group had risen, and now he was the one who wanted to be part of the inner circle. As I lay on my back looking up at the high roof and enjoying the sweet smell of hay, I sensed that I still had some things to take care of. I had still sores to be healed—and Wolfgang was one of them.

That night I noticed a few of the boys huddled in a corner, and as I strolled over I caught the glint of metal and saw a revolver passing from hand to hand. Herr Grothe had forbidden us to carry any weapons into the train or the barn. But the armed forces, it seemed, had simply dropped them when the war ended. Guns and ammunition could be found almost anywhere.

Suddenly a shot tore through the silence. Richard shrieked, grabbed his thigh, and fell over. Blood began to stain the hay and dirt on the floor. Chaos followed. Herr Grothe delivered a hasty lecture. Then there was silence again. The wife of one of the teachers had managed to remove the bullet and patched Richard up as well as she could.

It dawned on me that Richard, the strongest of the Food Search Commandoes, could no longer pull the cart. We'd have to find someone else.

Apparently the same thought came to Wolfgang. "What are you going to do now that Richard can't walk?" he whispered to me in the dark.

"Oh, he'll walk again." I said it casually.

"I mean tomorrow. What will you do?" he pressed.

"Well, we'll just have to find a substitute." I knew what was coming next and wasn't sure how I'd handle it.

"Reinhold, I know I've been pretty mean to you in the past. I'm sorry for all that. Do you think you could choose me? I'd really like to be part of the group."

I looked at the outline of the boy on the blanket a few feet from me. This was the chance I'd waited for for many months, but now I wouldn't be able to see his face.

At the same time I remembered the day we had lifted the ban and began speaking to him again after several weeks. He had come alive in seconds, and much of the bragging and belligerency I'd disliked had drained out of him. The fleeting desire I had to get even with him ebbed, and I told him, still somewhat reluctantly, "I'll talk to Herr Grothe. I think it can be arranged—at least as long as Richard can't walk."

He reached for my hand and pressed it. "Thank you, Reini. Thank you, friend."

I was moved but he couldn't see it in the dark. When he called me friend, I knew he meant it, and I had the beautiful feeling of beginning a friendship that might last.

Wolfgang proved to be a real asset to the team. Actually the job became a little easier. We had mastered the guttural Austrian dialect and stood in the long bakery lines for bread. The local farmers had gotten used to our presence and as the weather got warmer, the barn became a comfortable place to live.

Not everyone gave up his precious foodstuffs easily, though. We stopped at a dairy-cheese factory one morning, and I pleaded with the manager to sell us some food. I was willing to pay a goodly sum for either cheese or butter, but he coldly brushed us off.

When we walked out of his office, Juergen eyed three cases of butter at the far end of the hall and pointed. "Hey, wouldn't that be something?"

We knew what he meant. It would be easy to slip several pounds under our coats and be off.

"And how would you explain the butter to Herr Grothe?" I asked him.

"Well, we wouldn't have to take it back. We could eat it on the way."

I could feel the shock and anger register through the group. Had Juergen really suggested that we steal food?

To bridge the awkward silence I said, "I don't think you know what you're saying. This is a hand-picked team chosen for its honesty, and you want to break that trust?"

I could see that he felt badly, and he laughed it off. A moment later when we found a washroom at the end of the same hall, Richard and Wolfgang and I went in, but Juergen waited outside. I thought it was because of his embarrassment.

We started back to camp a little early that day and stopped at a dugout we had discovered with a camouflaged antiaircraft gun. In an instant we were transformed from responsible adults to children and for an hour or so lost ourselves in our own version of war. As we clambered over the giant weapon, blasting the imaginary Americans out of the way, a large spot of grease began to appear on Juergen's coat.

Wolfgang noticed it first and grabbed him. "Hey, man. What've you got there?"

Juergen pulled away but he was no match for Wolfgang. We stripped his coat off and found the pound of butter he had slipped inside.

"I'm sorry, Reinhold. Really. I'm sorry. I just couldn't resist it."

Not knowing how to handle it and still shaken by the incident, I said nothing, just looked at him. Unable to communicate with us, he turned and ran off toward camp.

When we arrived, Herr Grothe called me to his room. He was more subdued than usual and I knew something had happened.

"I don't know how you do it, Reinhold." He shook his head. "Juergen has made a full confession and I'm going to forgive him."

Forgive? I don't think I'd ever heard Herr Grothe use that term before.

"However, this is your last trip."

So he hadn't really forgiven and Juergen had dragged us all down with him. But Herr Grothe went on.

"Tomorrow we'll be picked up by buses and taken back to Germany. I don't know where, but I'm almost certain it won't be Berlin. I want to thank you for your work as commando leader. Without your team we might all have starved to death."

It was my turn to be subdued. This was a different Herr Grothe than I had ever known.

"You're welcome!" was all I could get out.

I walked back to the barn and stretched out on my blanket. If Herr Grothe had forgiven Juergen, I would, too. It was a small thing and almost forgotten already in the excitement of the news that we'd be back in Germany soon. I had a lot to be thankful for. Many of the boys had succumbed to apathy and some had died. The daily effort of searching for food, however, had kept my team alert and healthy—and alive.

Disappointment came quickly the next day. Packed

124

into rusty old army buses, we bumped a mere two hours over mountain roads, a few kilometers outside the town of Wagrain. We were still in Austria, short of the German border and relegated to some old army barracks. They were cramped and cold, without a stick of furniture, and—we soon learned—crawling with lice.

Without the Food Search Commandoes we had little to do during the days and I became bored and a little despondent. I suppose that's why, one evening, I agreed to join the group that was planning to raid a farmer's apple trees.

After lights went out that night, we inched open a window, crawled out, and, in pajamas and bare feet, dashed the two hundred meters to the orchards. We had tied our pajama legs with string, and we dumped the apples in and clumsily trotted back to the barracks. Climbing into a window with your pants full of apples is an awkward trick. Some of the stolen fruit dropped on the wooden floor.

Just as we got through the window, a light went on at the end of the row. We hit the floor where we were, grabbed any blanket available, and pretended to be sleeping. It was Herr Grothe, groping his way out to the latrine, and he didn't notice anything wrong. When he had gone and we had crawled back to our own blankets, Wolfgang whispered to me, "We would have lied."

"What?" I stammered, although I knew just what he meant.

"You know. If we were caught we would have lied."

"And just what would we say, that we had made the apples out of stones—like a magician?"

"No, like Jesus. Stones into bread."

He thought his remark was witty and he giggled, but it hit me differently. Like Jesus. I knew that story well. Satan had tempted Jesus to transform a stone to a loaf of bread. But Jesus suffered the ache of hunger instead of giving in to the devil's urging.

And, I thought, he wouldn't have stolen apples either.

"Wolfgang. Do you want my apples?" I asked suddenly.

"Are you crazy? You stole with us, now if we're caught you'll hang with us."

For a long time I lay there, the stolen apples close to me, my conscience keeping me from sleep.

"Juergen?" I rolled over the other way and whispered. "Are you asleep?"

"Yes, and I'm snoring," he cracked.

"We've been out stealing apples."

"I know."

"Why didn't you come?" I knew the answer even as I asked.

"Remember the butter?" He emphasized the word.

I felt shame creeping over me and I was glad it was dark. What a hypocrite! I had been so self-righteous before Juergen and Wolfgang and Herr Grothe. How could I ever explain it? Would they understand? I didn't know, but I quietly crept to the center of the room and put my apples on the floor. Whoever wanted them could take them. I wanted somehow to purge myself of this whole affair.

The first thing I heard the next morning was Herr Grothe's raspy voice:

"Well, what a miracle! You'd expect the apples to fall close to the tree."

He picked up three or four and tried to grasp another one but it kept slipping away.

"Keep shaking, boys. Keep shaking. I'll be back."

Almost immediately two other teachers appeared and the last apple disappeared in seconds.

When the teachers had gone, relief flooded the room

and most of the boys laughed. But I could see confusion in Juergen's eyes. I moved closer to him and whispered, "Never mind. There's still honesty in the world."

"Yeah, like where and who?" he cracked.

"Well, like my father," I blurted.

"Oh yeah!" He seemed skeptical.

Suddenly I said, "Look, Juergen, you stole that butter because you were hungry, but we stole the apples because we enjoyed stealing. I think that's worse."

I could see he was still troubled and confused. "I don't think it's the butter or the apples," he said slowly. "What bothers me is the teachers. They knew the apples were stolen. You'd think at least they'd be honest."

Then I knew just what to say, the only answer. "You're right about my father. I'm sure he's been dishonest sometime in his life. All of us are. But there is someone who will never disappoint you—Jesus Christ."

I wondered how he'd respond so I stopped, but he waited for me to go on.

"Jesus said, 'I am the way, the truth, and the life.' So if he's truth, then he's also honest. You see?"

"Is that in the Bible?"

"Yes! I don't know just where, but I learned that verse in Sunday school and I believe it."

"I've never been in Sunday school," he said softly, "but I believe it, too."

XV

When I began the third grade, our religion teacher announced that he would not tell us those stories about the cruel Jewish God or that meek and mild Jesus. Instead he would teach us about our original gods—Thor and Zeus and others, the gods of the old Germanic tribes from which our nation sprang. I was appalled. Even in my youthful understanding, this was going too far.

That was, perhaps, the earliest recollection I have of direct teaching about a super race. But the Reich used every means available to promote the doctrine. At our Monday night Hitler Youth meetings, we heard dreadful stories of so-called Jewish barbarities. Official speeches, magazines, newspapers, pictures, laws, acts of government—all helped to infuse in me the concept of the pure, strong, superior Aryan, in contrast to the weak, depraved, and inferior Jew or black man.

When the Third Reich fell, the myth of racial superiority fell with it. But I had yet to learn how deeply this insidious teaching had worked its way into my life. On the other hand, I still had plenty of room to experience God's grace and his power to heal.

We had spent an idle summer roaming the alpine valleys, drinking from the icy brooks, picking berries, or lying on our backs staring up at the mountains. Meals were regular but meager—two slices of bread for breakfast, a thin smelly soup for lunch, and two more slices of bread again at night.

We were about to dunk our dry bread in water early one September morning in 1945 when an American officer in a jeep stopped outside and ordered us to be ready to leave in thirty minutes.

"I need the barracks for my troops," he told us. Well, he could have his barracks. We really didn't care.

In half an hour two open army trucks appeared, and what was left of our school—students, teachers, blankets, a few books, and other goods—was pushed aboard. Only as we started north toward Salzburg did we learn that this time we were really going to Germany.

Before we got to the border, however, we had a small accident, and one of the drivers broke his arm trying to prop up the wheels of his truck.

Just then another military truck came up behind us, and two mammoth, black GIs jumped out and ran toward us.

I had only seen black-skinned soldiers from a distance, but I had heard all about them. In political instruction class we had heard terrifying stories of atrocities, human sacrifice, and devil worship.

We watched the two men carefully. They made a sling for the injured driver, then picked him up and carried

130

him to their truck. Next they hauled out a chain and pulled our truck out of the ditch. While they performed this Good Samaritan act, they kept up a light and friendly banter.

Gradually we realized that we had swallowed the big lie once again, and our fear turned to admiration. Here were two beautiful human beings helping us. And to think that I had been taught to fear all black men. I wondered how long—a lifetime, perhaps—the relentless propaganda of my childhood would hold sway over my heart and mind.

Shortly after that we crossed the frontier and touched German soil, shouting and repeating over and over again, *Deutschland, Deutschland*—as though saying the word out loud would keep the country from disappearing.

We had heard that our country was in ruins, burned out, impoverished, and its people homeless. But in this untouched corner of Bavaria we saw only blue sky, cattle grazing on the hill, and wild flowers stirring in the breeze. We weren't home yet, but this was the happiest and teariest day we had known for years.

Tyrlaching, our destination, had refused the Nazi order to defend itself against the American army. Instead they had run to the second-floor bedrooms, thrown open the windows, and surrendered amidst a sea of flapping white bedsheets.

The American soldiers did not live up to their image of being liberators, however. They refused food to begging children, forced the farmers' horses off the road and would not fraternize. As a final indignity they spread straw on the floor of the local dance hall and turned it into a stable.

That stable became our new home, and while the strong odor of dung permeated the room, we had beds and mattresses for the first time in months and, to our amazement, a meal with all the food we could eat. The owner of the inn invited us to his restaurant and sat us down at tables with real dishes. Then he assured us we'd have three good meals a day.

He went on with announcements, but my mind wandered. Three regular meals, a full stomach, a table, a bed. What did it matter that it was in a stable? Jesus was born in a stable, and he didn't even have a bunkbed. I felt especially close to him that night, praying and reading his Word at the end of my first eventful day back in Germany.

On Hitler's birthday, April 20, the citizenry of Berlin and any other German who could manage to get there would throng the square outside the Reich Chancellery on the Wilhelmstrasse. It was a grand day with bands and military parades and speeches. Like the pope, Hitler would appear on a small balcony, and smile on the masses, and they would shout, "heil, heil, heil," until they were hoarse.

I remember going there as a boy, sitting on my father's shoulders to catch a glimpse of the *Fuehrer*—"the Leader." It was the greatest experience a small boy could have.

Many people have tried to explain Hitler's hold on the German people. They've written about his eyes, his hypnotic effect, his magnetism. Without a doubt he captured the soul of a suffering nation in the early thirties and parlayed that popularity into no less than a God-image.

After I learned the truth, I was unaware that a mass of unresolved anger and resentment had begun to build and simmer deep inside me.

That probably accounted for my extraordinary behavior one September afternoon. Our gang had gone to the fair in a neighboring town. A group of Bavarian boys waited until we got off of the ferris wheel and, in front of a gaggle of laughing girls, beat us to the ground and pounded us. It was humiliating and frustrating because we were outnumbered, and we had no choice but to drag ourselves back to Tyrlaching.

We didn't feel like going back to the stables, so we stopped at one of the ponds on the edge of town and vented our feelings by throwing rocks.

I don't know who had the idea first, but we all saw the cat at the same time, and in seconds we surrounded her and caught her.

"Hey, let's scalp her," Werner cried. We had played a lot of cowboys and Indians in the last few weeks. Every German boy had read the books of Karl May, who had written about the plight of the American Indians. We had spent hours acting out his stories.

"Stupid, she doesn't have enough hair for that."

"Then let's cut her whiskers off."

That sounded reasonable, so with Juergen's pocket knife, we trimmed the black hairs while the animal squirmed.

It was then that I noticed the resemblance and I shouted, "She looks like Adolf Hitler."

Startled, the boys took a second look, then laughed.

"You're right! She even has a brown shirt on," Richard added.

"Let's drown her."

The words jumped out before I knew what I was saying. We found an old sack nearby, and even though it had holes in it, we managed to get the poor animal in and tie it up. We added a few stones for weight, then Wolfgang took it and flung it as far as he could into the pond.

For a moment the jerking bundle floated, then it slowly sank. We stood and cheered. But suddenly a wet, brown head appeared on the surface. Hitler was loose.

In a frenzy we scrambled for stones and began to bombard the figure. An unreal fear gripped me. What if Hitler swam to shore and attacked us? I saw the black whiskers and brown shirt coming closer, and in a mad rage I threw one stone after another until one hit the cat squarely on the forehead. For a second she stopped paddling, then she disappeared.

Still shaking I turned to see Richard, Wolfgang, Werner, and Juergen doing a mock Indian war dance. It had been a game for them, a boyish prank in which, perhaps, they could vent their feelings of anger from earlier that afternoon. But that act of violence had not been play for me. I had purposefully drowned the whiskers and brownshirt. I had symbolically killed the mustachioed Hitler—and I felt no remorse.

I had always loved cats, but in drowning this one I rid myself of the hurt and disappointment that Hitler had inflicted on me. He had betrayed my faith. He had cheated my heart—and the poor cat died for it.

I was still staring at the water when the others started to leave.

"You coming?" one of them asked.

"No! Don't wait for me."

"She's not coming up again."

I knew that, but I continued to stare. Then I bent down and looked at the face of a fourteen-year-old German boy in the water. In movies I had seen murderers shy away from the sight of their own face, but I didn't even blink. I was no murderer. A killer, perhaps. But it felt good, so good, to get Adolf Hitler out of my life once and for all.

XVI

We very quickly grew accustomed to three good meals
a day. The time of going without food for several days
seemed like a bad dream. By the end of September,
however, the days were shorter and colder and we
needed warm clothing. Our teachers asked the American officer in charge, the village clerk, even the villagers, but no one had anything for us.

I spent many hours those days reading my Bible. By
now my classmates had accepted the fact that one of
them was a religious "fanatic," but none of them
mocked me anymore. For one thing, Richard, the
biggest one among us, had become my defender. An
uncomplimentary reference to my Bible reading or
praying brought a glare from Richard, and the offender
backed off quickly.

One evening Herr Grothe decided we should try to

write letters home.

"I don't know if there's any mail service to Berlin, but at least you should try," he encouraged us.

I had carefully saved the letters I had received back in Czechoslovakia. The last one had been postmarked more than six months ago. All I had for my father was a military address, but there was no military any longer, so I addressed a letter to my mother in Berlin.

That night I prayed very hard that God would let me find my parents. Then I thumbed through the Bible, trying to find some comfort, some passage that would speak especially to me at the moment.

For some reason I stopped at the sixth chapter of 1 Corinthians and started to read:

"All things are lawful for me, but not all things are helpful. All things are lawful for me but I will not be enslaved by anything."

It didn't seem to have anything to do with my problem then, so I skipped on:

"The body is not meant for immorality, but for the Lord, and the Lord for the body. . . . Do you not know that your bodies are members of Christ."

I kept skipping and reading, even though it said nothing special to me.

"But he who is united to the Lord becomes one spirit with him. Shun immorality. Every other sin which a man commits is outside the body; but the immoral man sins against his own body. Do you not know that your body is the temple of the Holy Spirit within you, which you have from God? You are not your own, you were bought with a price. So glorify God in your body."

I put the Bible down, disappointed, but then began to think about the words. I had seen immorality around me. For months we had lived with almost around-the-clock body contact, and I had often seen boys showing

136

sexual desires toward other boys. In Tyrlaching immorality seemed to have broken loose with force. The bathroom was the scene of many acts that made me complete my business and hurry out of there.

As I was running this around in my mind, Herr Grothe turned the lights off, and Juergen, in the bunk above me, began to whisper to me. I jumped up to sit beside him and continue the conversation, but I was so involved in the topic that I didn't notice his unusual friendliness. He hadn't touched me in any indecent way, but I understood the precariousness of my situation when he asked,

"What do you think our parents would say if they saw us here together?"

Had I been blind and dumb? Had my long and innocent friendship with Juergen lulled me to trust him when I should have seen the warning signs?

Without a word, I slipped off his bed, pulled the blankets off of mine in the bunk below and moved to an empty bed a few bunks away.

"What's the matter? Hey, Reinhold, where're you going?"

I ignored his pleading and lay there shivering. Then the words came back to me. "Shun immorality!" I had done that even at the expense of my treasured friendship with Juergen. "So glorify God in your body." I wanted to do that. I desperately wanted to, but it was difficult at times.

The next day I began to read my Bible again, searching for a passage I had read that stuck in the back of my mind. Finally I found it in Romans.

"Though they know God's decree that those who do such things deserve to die, they not only do them but approve those who practice them." Paul was writing about "men who were consumed with passion for one another, men committing shameless acts with men."

As I read I realized that the hours of reading and studying the Bible were more than a way to pass time. For years I had received instruction from my father or a pastor or Sunday school teacher. I had taken their admonitions and tried to live by them. Now I had read and understood and applied the Word of God on my own. It was an important lesson. I had listened to my father and marvelled so many times at his understanding of the Bible. He always seemed to have the right passage for the right time. It was as though the Word was a part of him, and although he might read the words off the page to me, he seemed to be reaching down within himself to pull them out. He'd be pleased, I knew, but I realized with a pang even as I thought it that I couldn't tell him. I had no idea where he was.

Early one morning in October, the mother of one of the boys arrived from Berlin. She had a petition that many parents had signed to get their sons back home, and we crowded around her to see whose name was on it. For the last several weeks mail had begun to trickle through, but I hadn't received anything. So I held up the list and carefully checked each name. Then I saw it: Hedwig Kerstan. The signature turned blurry as I stared at it. My eyes filled with tears and I began to cry.

"My mother lives!" I whispered over and over again. No longer did I feel lonely and forgotten. A dozen or more boys from our class had already been picked up by their parents. Each time one of them had left I set my teeth so as not to cry in disappointment. Waiting for mail each day had been nerve-racking. But now I knew, and the world turned a brighter hue, even through my tear-filled eyes.

"Will you take me with you . . . back to Berlin," I

pleaded with the woman who had brought the petition.

"No, no, I can't. But we'll give this list to the military authorities. They'll let you go soon."

She didn't understand, of course. The military authorities had already fingerprinted us and marked on our identification papers that we were not to leave Tyrlaching. Unless someone kidnapped me, I thought, I'd have to sit here and grow old. After being lifted so high, it was a hard drop. But I had something to cling to that I hadn't had before—I knew my mother was alive.

The woman and her son were gone the next morning before I had a chance to say goodbye, but now the ache and the loneliness were gone. I had something to live for no matter how long I had to wait.

Late one afternoon after we had played a hard day at cowboys and Indians, two more mothers arrived to collect their sons, and the word was out that they would take several more along. I refused to get excited, however. There were still thirty or forty boys in camp, and I had very little chance of being chosen. I didn't know these mothers and I tried to avoid meeting them. The tearful reunions made me long for my mother's arrival, and I didn't want to risk the disappointment of being left out again.

At supper I couldn't resist, however, and went over to look at the list of names they had. Neither my mother's name nor mine was on it, and, hardly caring whether I ate or not, I sat down at one of the tables. My soul was in an uproar. I had prayed, day after day, that I could go home. Why wouldn't God answer my prayers? For some reason snatches of Psalm 73 kept coming to mind. My father had insisted that we memorize it when I was small, and now I thought I understood it:

> Truly God is good to the upright,
> to those who are pure in heart.

But as for me, my feet had almost stumbled,
my steps had well nigh slipped.
For I was envious of the arrogant,
when I saw the prosperity of the wicked.
For they have no pangs;
Their bodies are sound and sleek.
They are not in trouble as other men are;
They are not stricken like other men . . .
They set their mouths against the heavens,
and their tongue struts through the earth . . .
Therefore the people turn and praise them;
and find no fault in them.
And they say, "How can God know?
Is there knowledge in the most high?"
Behold these are the wicked;
always at ease they increase their riches. . . .

Then I couldn't remember any more of the Psalm, only that the writer complained to God that he had kept his hands and heart clean, but it all seemed so useless because others had done the opposite and gotten ahead. Well, I had tried, while. . . .

"Kerstan!" Herr Grothe's voice broke through and he looked at me sharply.

"Isn't that your name? Kerstan?"

"Yes, it is." He hardly ever called me that, so I didn't understand.

"All right, then. Come up here and stand with these ladies."

Then it struck me. I was one of those chosen to go along with them. I jumped up and ran toward them.

"Will I be going with you? Will you take me along?"

Everyone laughed because that's what they had been talking about while I daydreamed over the Psalm.

"Yes, Reinhold, you'll come with us." Mrs. Bilker put her arm around me. "We promised your mother we'd bring you."

140

I closed my eyes, then opened them slowly to make sure the woman was still there. Now that the long-awaited day had come, I felt a tired relief rather than a whooping and shouting joy. And I knew there were others left who would have to wait without knowing how long.

We spent the evening making plans—the time we'd leave, the route we'd take, the provisions we'd pack, what we'd say and not say to the patrols. (We didn't have the right papers and could easily get stopped at the first train station.) The next day was October 31. We rested as much as we could for the journey. Finally darkness came, and it was time to leave.

XVII

Was I really on my way home? And how far did we
expect to get without the right papers? Today you can
drive the distance from Tyrlaching to Berlin in eight
hours on the autobahn. With luck, if we made it at all,
we expected to arrive in five or six days.

Our band of nine—Mrs. Bilker, Mrs. Becker, their
two sons, and five more of us—began walking shortly
after midnight to reach the station in Laufen by dawn.
No sooner had we arrived and bought tickets, however,
than the American Military Police appeared to check
papers. Neither of the women spoke a word of English,
so they shoved our tickets and the letters of authoriza-
tion from our mothers under the noses of the policemen
and jabbered away. The Americans did not know
enough German to understand a word of what they
said.

At the same time the verses from Psalm 23 began

going through my head.

The Lord is my shepherd, I shall lack nothing.
He makes me lie down in green pastures.

As I repeated them, I felt at ease. I didn't understand why, but it didn't make any difference. My anxiety gradually flowed out of me.

He leads me beside the still waters,
He restores my soul.

Finally the MPs pushed the papers back to us, smiled and saluted casually, then turned to the next passenger on the platform.

Surely goodness and mercy will follow me all the days of my life.

"What's that, Reinhold?" Richard, who was part of our group, looked at me strangely as I mumbled.

"Nothing, friend, nothing. Let's get a little closer to the tracks so we can get a better seat."

We were free. Actually on our way home.

Even at that early hour and in that remote village, the station was crowded. Long before the train pulled in, more people than I ever thought could get on lined the platform. Finally our small group with about ten others jammed into a compartment that had been built for eight. We were on our way.

Our tickets were good to Augsburg, but our train only went as far as Munich and there were no more trains leaving Munich that day. What a blow to our hopes! The railroad station was cold and damp with hundreds of people sitting around, trying to sleep, playing cards, eating. We took turns guarding the luggage while the others went to look at the city, but the rubble-filled streets and ruined buildings so depressed us that we picked our way back to the station. We settled as best we could for the night on a clear spot on the concrete floor.

144

Early the next morning we pushed into another overcrowded compartment on a train to Nuremberg. This time I could see out through a hole in the plywood that had been nailed over the broken train window. I passed the time by counting damaged locomotives, blown-up bridges, and burnt-out raiload cars. In a half day my friend Wolfgang and I counted eighty-nine locomotives, twenty-eight bridges, and several hundred cars before we tired of the game.

We spent the second night in the Nuremberg train station, counting ourselves fortunate that we at least had wooden benches to stretch out on.

No one slept much. Children cried and adults talked loudly. Some people had brought pots and cooked on the station floor over open fires. The odors, mingled with cheap tobacco smoke, made it hard to breathe. Hardly an inch of floor space remained, making it difficult to hopscotch around the station when we did have to move.

Toward morning a freight train with open cars pulled in and we joined the shouting and pushing crowd for the platform. We managed to get all nine of us onto one car only to find that the train was loaded with coal. For the next ten hours we sat on hard lumps, engulfed in black dust, shivering in the November wind, but we were happy to be on our way again, this time toward Frankfurt. It wasn't a direct route, but each stop brought us just a little closer to Berlin.

Actually we had no business riding the trains. Only passengers with special permits from the military government were allowed to travel, but the crowds were desperate and determined, and pity the poor railway official who tried to stop them.

At the East Frankfurt station, we learned we'd have to walk across the city to the main station. The city was hardly recognizable. Only a path through the ruins marked what had once been a thriving commercial center.

From Frankfurt we rode—rather stood—in the gangway of a coach train to Marburg, about a three-hour ride. Then we spent one more night on cold cement, this time outside the station building. In the morning I awoke to find snow settling softly on my blanket and head.

Snow! Why did it have to snow? That would mean tracks when we crossed the border into the Russian zone. Oh Lord, why did it have to snow?

From Marburg we found a train to Kassel, and, to our amazement, it had heat. There we boarded a train to Goettingen, then another one to Braunschweig.

Gradually we grew accustomed to the sight of destruction. Every city looked the same—frightened old people, hollow-eyed children wandering through the debris, hastily built shelters, and the stench of death. The war had ended six months ago, and winter would grip the country within weeks. I shuddered, vaguely sensing the hard times to come.

We planned to cross into the Russian zone just before Helmstedt, but without papers we couldn't do that on the train. Many others, we learned, had followed the same route, and a clever businessman ran a truck from Braunchweig to an isolated spot on a country road near the border. It was close to midnight when we got off the truck and started walking.

"It's a good night to cross," Mrs. Bilker whispered. "It's going to snow and it's hard to see."

After that, no one said anything until the crowd with us began to break off into the fields on both sides of the road. We followed the two women across a ploughed field, stumbling and tripping until we reached the edge

146

of a wood.

"Hey, Reini? You praying?" Wolfgang spoke softly in my ear.

"Have been all day."

He squeezed my arm.

I didn't feel as brave as I sounded, and I wondered if Mrs. Becker and Mrs. Bilker really knew what they were doing. Was the border close? And what about the guards and dogs? Or landmines? The woods gave us more cover, but the branches scratched our faces. Mrs. Becker slipped, pulling Richard down with her, and they both fell face first into a creek that was partially covered with leaves and snow. They came up icy cold and shivering, but we couldn't stop then to dry them out.

Without warning a black form loomed in front of us, and an enormous dog threw himself at Mrs. Becker. We stood paralyzed, waiting for a guard to appear, but no one came. Then the dog let go of the woman and came bounding toward me.

"It's the bread," Richard hissed. "The bread in your knapsack."

With shaking hands I unbuckled the pack, slipped it off and opened it. I had saved half a loaf for my mother, but without a thought of her I broke off a chunk for the animal.

Richard was right, and while the dog chewed, we pushed on. He caught up with us twice, and I finally gave him the last piece of my bread.

"Let's run," Mrs. Bilker urged us as we emerged into a clearing. The dog, wagging his tail and enjoying the sport, bounded ahead of us, and as we neared more woods we heard voices.

"It's that crazy dog again."

"Why doesn't someone shoot him?"

147

One voice spoke in clear German, and the other had a pronounced Russian accent.

We kept on running, and when we could run no longer, we stopped. The dog had run off, and we could see the hard outline of houses through the dark. After a few more meters, we found a road, then a sign with the name of the village. Beneath it in handpainted letters were the words *Russische Besatzungzone*—Russian Occupied Zone.

We had made it! We had crossed half the country without travel permits, and now we had crossed into the Russian Zone.

All we had to do now was find a ride to Berlin.

In comparison with what we had gone through, the next leg was easy. A friendly railroad official helped us get on a train to Magdeburg, and after another cold night in a railroad station we boarded a train for Berlin.

I was in a frenzy now that I was so close. I watched the towns pass, impatient for some familiar landscape. I knew what Berlin looked like, and I wouldn't rest until I saw something I recognized. I was almost home!

As the train made one of its interminable stops, I pulled my nose from the window for a moment and turned to see Wolfgang, his head back on the cushion, his eyes closed, tears pouring down his cheeks.

"Wolfgang. . . . What is it?"

He continued to sob, and I reached over and touched his hand. After a few minutes he began to tell me his story.

His mother and father had been divorced, and while his mother worked in the chocolate factory he had been a *Schluesselkind*—a kid with the key to his house on a string around his neck.

"Soon my mother began bringing other men home. I had to call them all 'Uncle,' but I hated them. We always

148

had candy around the house, but that was the only good thing.

"Camp was like paradise to me, until you came and got all those letters from home. I hated you. I was jealous that you came from a family that cared for each other. It was when you put me under the ban that I began to pray."

"You what?" I wasn't sure I had heard him correctly.

As we talked about it, he also mentioned the time they had crucified me to the bed post.

"You didn't know it, but that's the day I decided to live for Jesus," I told him. "I figured that you were going to make fun of me anyhow, so I might as well live like a Christian."

He was quiet for a moment, then mused, "Richard was the smartest one. He said if we pushed you too far, we'd push you right back to God."

Good old Richard! I looked over at him, but he had fallen asleep. He had given me many signs of his friendship, but the pressure of the group had kept him from taking an openly Christian stand.

As the train neared the city, I shared my faith in Christ with Wolfgang and told him about the simple steps he would have to take to know he'd go to heaven.

"It sure sounds easy to get to hell," Richard broke in. We hadn't noticed that he was awake and had probably been listening for some time.

We were now entering the suburbs of Berlin. As far as I could see, they hadn't changed much. Closer in, however, the destruction grew worse. Soon I saw nothing but ruins, burned-out factories, roofs blown away, walls ready to topple.

At the Zoologischer Garten station, we got off. The two mothers helped us find the right subway connection. In a matter of minutes Richard and I stood on the platform alone.

While I was trying to board the train to Neukoelln, however, we were separated, and I was unable to share my faith with him any further.

The crowds seemed possessed—screaming, pounding with their fists, many more people than could ever get on the train. Twice I almost lost my knapsack as it was pulled along faster than I could work my way after it.

At last I was on the train, alone, yet surrounded by hundreds of people.

How good it was to be in familiar territory once again! From Gleisdreieck to Boddinstrasse was six stops. I thought I had enough strength left to stand, if only I could get through the wall of people and out of the car at the right time. I counted off the stops, then began to push with my last reserve of energy. Somehow, the mass opened up, and I was literally ejected onto the platform.

Upstairs on the street I stopped and looked around, surprised and incredulous to find that not much had changed. My old school, the Lettow Vorbeck High School, had been bombed, and the trees in the park were mostly gone, but otherwise it looked just as I had left it.

I walked the last one hundred meters and tried to get the shaking out of my knees. At number 45 I stopped. There was a lump in my throat.

In my daydreaming I had often seen myself run up those steps to our apartment door and almost break in. Now I dragged myself up slowly, anxiety building with each familiar tread. I touched the wooden railing gently, took in the smell of the hallway, and finally stood before the solid oakwood door to my home.

XVIII

Siegfried opened the door, gaped for a second, then ran back into the house shouting, "Mutti, Mutti, Reinhold is here." The next moment I was enclosed in the warmth of my mother's arms and our tears mingled as we clung to each other.

"Mein Junge, mein Junge," she repeated over and over again.

"I'm sorry, Mutti, a dog ate the bread I had saved for you."

She smiled and wiped her watery eyes and nodded, not understanding what I was talking about.

"It's okay, it's okay! You're home, *mein Junge.*"

As I opened my pack to pull out the few items I'd managed to hold on to for months, I realized that it would take many weeks, perhaps months, if it were ever possible, to explain all that had happened to me in the time I had been away—Herr Grothe's tight, sadistic control at the Villa Fragner, the dive bombers and the partisans, Horst and Tim, Captain Davis, the Food Search Commandoes, the Fuehrer cat. . . .

I dumped the contents of my worn and dirty pack on the carpet and looked up, puzzled. "Where's Vati?"

Siegfried and my mother looked at each other and their smile vanished. "Didn't you know? Your father was sent to the front in Italy. We haven't heard from him since before the end of the war."

Not home? Haven't heard from him? Well, we would in time. My father had to come home.

Meanwhile, I couldn't keep my head up and my eyes open. Would my mother mind if I stretched out on the carpet for a few minutes? It felt so good to stretch out all the way on something warm and soft.

I awoke fourteen hours later in the only bed I had seen in the apartment.

There was so much to catch up on. Siegfried was back in school. He had been drafted into the army near the end.

"And now I'm as glad as I was sorry then," my mother threw in. "Who knows what might have happened to him here in Berlin. Did you hear about the Wolters boys?"

No, I hadn't heard about them.

When the Russians came close to our district, Neukoelln, a military official came and conscripted them instantly into a defensive army. Her three sons, along with more than three hundred Hitler Youth, died defending the city hall.

I knew Mrs. Wolters and her three boys, and I quickly began to talk of other things. I already had a long list of names of slain boys etched in my mind, and I didn't want to add more. In a few days I'd be fourteen. I had

152

missed something someplace, some carefree years, some slow growing and maturing as a young boy. I had been thrust into adulthood, and I felt old.

I had heard enough about the grimness of life in Berlin to know that it wouldn't be like it was before I left. Nevertheless I was shocked to see people searching for food in garbage cans. I had seen it in Frankfurt and Kassel and other cities, but could it really happen in Berlin?

On the third day home, mother and I went to a government office to try to get a ration card for me. After three offices and many hours, all we got was a reprimand.

"You should have known better, Mrs. Kerstan, than to bring your son back illegally!"

Meanwhile I'd have to wait and share the four thin slices of bread my mother and brother received.

Well, I might be hungry, but at least I was home—what was left of it. Half the wall to the neighboring apartment had fallen, and a huge wardrobe stood in the gap. It blocked the view, but it didn't stop the sounds from the bedroom beyond it. The wall between the living room and our bedroom had also fallen down. In fact, only the kitchen and my father's study seemed to have survived the bombing without much damage. The study, with the help of an old iron stove, was the only heated room, and my mother and brother had made that the living room-bedroom. It also had the only window with glass, a small peephole in the wood that had been nailed over most of the area.

Several days later I had completely forgotten any discomfort I might have noticed. My mother and brother woke me up early. I had turned fourteen, an important birthday for a German boy. From now on people would address me with "Sie" instead of the common "Du" used when speaking to children. And I could wear long pants.

My mother held a candle in her hands, and she had Siegfried sing the traditional birthday song, *Bis hierher hat dich Gott gebracht*—""God has guided you thus far." In kitchen they had put a paper streamer around my plate and allotted me two full slices of bread. Siegfried had found two pencils and an eraser, and Mother had managed to get three handkerchiefs. They had no wrapping paper, of course, so they hid the presents under homemade birthday cards. After breakfast the three of us knelt beside the table, thanked God for my homecoming, and asked for his blessing for the days ahead. What a wonderful way to begin such an important year of my life!

Most of my days were spent waiting in lines at government offices trying to break the barrier of official resistance and to get a ration card. Until then I couldn't even start back to school.

On one morning trip, I met Herr and Frau Grothe on the street. I hadn't seen them until they were directly in front of me, and, instinctively, I started to salute. Then I dropped my arm and instead extended it to shake hands and wished them good morning. We exchanged a few pleasantries, then went on. But I realized as they passed that my past feelings of resentment had gone completely. Back in Czechoslovakia and Austria, the boys had planned to report them for cruel and inhuman behavior. Now all I felt was a mixture of pity and indifference.

But I was glad I had met them because I knew then that they were part of the past. They were no longer part of my life. They were a sore that had been healed and could no longer threaten the health of my soul.

154

I still had not received my ration card by Christmas, but I had more time to think. The memory of last Christmas haunted me, and I wanted desperately to wipe it out with a celebration that honored Christ—not Adolf Hitler.

Last year Herr Grothe had sent Kurt out into the forest with three of the boys to find a tree. By that time the Czech partisans were attacking in open day light, and we feared for their safety. But in a few hours they were back with a giant fir tree that we placed in the entrance hall to the Villa.

Some kind of Christmas spirit touched Herr Grothe while we worked to raise the tree, but as soon as it was up he fell back into character.

"Go on, boys. Into the classroom to make ornaments. Now, to honor the Fatherland and our Fuehrer, we will decorate our tree with hundreds of little swastika flags. None of this nonsense about stars and angels and cribs."

I was disappointed at the time, and now, as I look back on it, I can see how perverted it was.

He made his stock speech about the glorious qualification and bright future of a Hitler Youth, then left us cutting up and painting the little red, white, and black flags.

"Why don't we sing a few Christmas carols?" I had asked Richard who was sitting next to me.

"Good idea, but don't ask me to begin."

To our amazement Kurt started us out and we joined in.

Stille Nacht, Heilige Nacht—"Silent night, holy night." We sang a second verse, then a third, before Herr Grothe came charging in.

"I hardly turn my back and you start singing those Jewish songs! What kind of Hitler Youth are you? Why can't you sing the beautiful new Christmas songs the

Fuehrer has given us?"

He ordered us out into the hall to put our swastikas on the tree, then told Kurt to lead us in singing the right songs. That was a disaster. Kurt, now in Herr Grothe's disfavor, tried, but we would not cooperate. Shaking his crippled fist and cursing us, he told us that all Christmas leaves had been cancelled because of our stubbornness; then he stomped away.

That was a year ago. This Christmas would be different.

In the midst of the rubble in our apartment I had found several boxes of Christmas glass balls, paper stars, and other ornaments. Finding a tree to put them on, however, was a different story. Every available branch and bush for miles had been cut down for firewood, but after days of searching, Siegfried and I found a few evergreen twigs and ran home with them. While we decorated them, Mother made a special potato cake, and we sang carols. There was no Herr Grothe to stop us this time, and when we sang "O Come All Ye Faithful" and "Joy to the World," we rejoiced. We had each other, food, a warm room to live in. We only wanted Father. Where was he this Christmas Eve?

It didn't bother us when the lights went out while we were singing. It gave us an excuse to burn five candles instead of one—a real luxury! My mother had a beautiful soprano voice, and she began to sing a song we'd never sung before at Christmas. Siegfried and I joined her, aware that it was the most fitting expression of what we felt that Christmas Eve:

Savior, like a shepherd lead us;
Much we need thy tender care.
In thy tender pastures feed us;
For our use thy folds prepare.
Blessed Jesus, blessed Jesus,

156

Thou hast bought us, thine we are.
Blessed Jesus, blessed Jesus
Thou hast bought us, thine we are.

Our church had met in a unit of our apartment complex, but in the winter of 1944 a parachute mine had landed on it. On Christmas morning we had to walk several kilometers to a school house that we used for worship until we could build a new church.

"Let's not forget to take three pieces of coal to keep us warm at church, one for each of us," my mother reminded us.

"We have only two pieces left." Siegfried gave her the bad news.

Mother paused for a moment, weighing the decision.

"All right! We'll take the two pieces. God will see to it that we have some for tomorrow." That settled it.

I had almost forgotten what it was like to worship with a church, but a few days after I arrived home I rediscovered the sense of belonging that I had known before.

On our arrival the pastor greeted us warmly. The room was almost full, but one row of worshipers squeezed together to make room for us.

I was startled when my mother and Siegfried bowed their heads to pray just as they sat down. What was I supposed to pray? Something special? I couldn't remember. So I began to pray for the people I knew in the service; for those, like my father, who hadn't returned from the war; for my heart and mind to be ready for the One who was invisibly present.

Yes, that was what it was for. I felt very much at home among God's people, and I wondered if Jesus had the same feeling when, at twelve, he visited the temple in Jerusalem. There he must have discovered that he was "in his own."

The gray-haired evangelist who was taking my father's place thanked the congregation for the gift of coal and used it as an illustration of the Christian life.

"When we are willing to share, God will make us so much richer for it. Just as you have brought together this pile of coal, so we have to bring others to Christ. One piece of coal would not warm us, but the effort and giving of many will keep us warm and alive. So it is with the life of the church. If we stay together we will be able to radiate warmth and life and will attract others who are about to die in loneliness."

XIX

A few days after New Year's, the Berlin authorities cleared me to live in the city, and I received a ration card. That also meant I could go to school.

Most of the school buildings were in ruins. Those that were open were run on a double shift to accommodate everyone. Classrooms were unheated, toilet facilities didn't work, windows were boarded up. When the electricity went off, school was held in the dark. We found some relief however, in the long central corridor. Because of the broken windows, the cement floor had accumulated a layer of ice. We turned it into a long slide and spent every free moment we could on it. Of course, there was some danger. The wall at the end of the corridor was missing, and if we didn't stop in time, we could drop four stories to the ground. For most of us, however, that risk was small compared to what we had gone through in the last year.

I was halfway down the slide one day when I saw Werner, and I made a daring jump off the ice to greet him.

"Hey, how've you been? When did you come back? Do you go to this school?"

"Good! Recently, and yes," he answered all three of my questions.

We hugged each other and laughed.

Still laughing, I asked him, "Did you find your parents okay?"

He looked at me and stopped smiling. "No, they're dead."

I couldn't conceal my shock. "You mean . . . you mean . . ." was all I could get out.

"You remember the telegram that Herr Grothe made me read?"

It all came back to me in an instant. Werner had read aloud to everyone the telegram saying that his parents were dead. We thought he was joking, but now for the first time I realized he wasn't.

"It was true. But I already knew it. My parents had told me they'd commit suicide if Germany lost the war."

The school bell rang, mercifully, making us both hurry off to class, but I promised him I'd stay in touch.

Most days after school Siegfried and I spent digging for wooden beams and boards or broken furniture to burn for fuel. We didn't have to go too far from our own apartment to find rubble. Since we had only one shovel and one ax, we worked together. When we dug something out, one of us would carry it back while the other stayed to guard the remaining pieces or to keep digging. When it got dark, we'd go home to warm up on soup, generally of an unknown composition, that

160

mother had made.

The day after Christmas I had gone down to the basement expecting to see more coal in the place of the two we had taken to church. In some way, I thought, perhaps by means of a miracle, God would replace them. I was disappointed, however, to find the bin empty. What had happened? Didn't God know of our need? We had given the last two pieces away for him and now we needed more.

The very next day Siegfried and I found two pieces of coal that had dropped off the back of a truck, plus a lot of twisted boards from an old floor.

The miracle had happened! God had used us. I wanted so very much for God to use me, and I knew that the wood under my arm was part of his miraculous plan to keep us alive. The following day I took two pieces of wood for the stove at school.

I thought that the days of not having enough to eat had ended when we arrived in Tyrlaching. But the familiar hollow feeling in my stomach returned almost as soon as I got back home to Berlin. The backbreaking work of digging through the rubble for wood made me even hungrier, and that made it more difficult to study.

One day when the pangs were too great, I pushed aside my books and said, "Mutti, I'm going skating."

"It's cold out and you've had nothing to eat. Stay and do your homework."

In her mind it was a contradiction to fight hunger with exercise. As soon as I was on the ice, however, gliding and gaining speed, rolling out in a long curve, I forgot my hunger—even my homework! Skating was my escape.

When I returned, though, I was hungrier than ever, and I pleaded, "Can I have just one slice of bread?"

161

"No, Reini, you cannot and you may not," Mother said, correcting my language at the same time.

"Mutti, I am very, very hungry."

"You should have thought of that before you went skating."

I tried one more time but she answered, "No, and no again. When I got that loaf I divided it into four parts so that it would last four days."

With that she put the bread in the kitchen cabinet and locked the door.

I was a little offended, and I declared,

"You don't have to lock it up. I wouldn't touch it without your permission."

"Are you sure, Reinhold?" She gave me one of her penetrating looks. "Marriages have split up. Parents and children have fought bitterly over food distribution. So far we've avoided that, but let's keep it that way by removing the temptation."

She was right. You can't trust anybody when it comes to hunger. People had fought and some were actually killed trying to get into the garbage cans of the American forces. Even digging for firewood was getting dangerous. Young boys had been beaten and their wood taken away by adults who put their own needs first.

I knew, of course, that within all of us is the capacity for unimaginable evil. "The heart is deceitful above all things. . . ." I had read that Bible verse many times. But I believed that the brutality and depravity that I had come to associate with the Nazi regime was now all a part of the past.

One day an old man riding a wooden cart with a bony horse came down the Boddinstrasse. He was collecting potato peels for which he offered wooden logs in exchange.

Nobody was taking up his offer, however, and he was

obviously tired and desperate. Anyone who had potatoes ate the skins. To go hungry was worse than to freeze.

Suddenly the old horse slipped and fell and as much as the man pulled and pushed, he couldn't get the horse up.

I had walked over to help him, and he asked me to stay with the horse while he went for a board to use as a lever.

"I'll go. I know the neighborhood," I started to say, but he was off.

He was no sooner gone when two men stood over the horse.

"He's dead," one of them said.

"Yea, too bad!" And with that the other man landed his fist on the horse's head. In a second they both had knives out and had stuck them into the neck and belly of the poor animal. The horse was far from dead, however, and began to kick wildly.

In spite of my protests, in the next few minutes, they finished killing the horse, then began cutting him up. A woman to whom I had turned for help also joined the men, pulling out an old scarf and wrapping a piece of the horse flesh in it. In less than a minute a crowd had gathered, and before the old man returned they had reduced his animal to a pile of bones and skin.

It came as a shock to see that butchering crowd kill to fill its bellies, but why should I expect people to change just because the reins of government had changed hands? There would still be war, for example. Even now the Russians and the Americans were lining up toe to toe right in Berlin, and World War III might begin any day.

Every evening after Siegfried and I had completed

our homework, Mother got out the thick family Bible and we read together, chapter after chapter. Those evenings when we had little or no electric light, we kept the readings short and the discussions long. That was when the Bible came alive to me in a way it never had before.

The Nazis had called the men of the Bible "the polluting scum of the earth," but they were my heroes. In spite of my admiration for the leaders of the Third Reich, I had never brought myself to dislike men such as Moses, Abraham, Jacob, David. Himmler, Goebbels, Goering—these self-proclaimed heroes—were either in prison or dead, whereas the Old Testament prophets were more alive than they had ever been to me.

But where was my father? Not an evening passed but we prayed for his safe return.

Then one day a frail-looking man in old army clothes much too large for him stood at our apartment door. Our father, he told us, was the chaplain of a POW camp in Italy and would probably be released soon.

Father was alive! It was the first news we had had for more than a year. We showered the bearer of good news with what little food we had, urged him to stay with us, even sleep in our bed, but he was anxious to get home to his own family, and after a few hours he left.

Several weeks later, without warning, I opened the door to the ringing of the bell and looked up into the face of my father. Rather than call for the family, I threw myself at him, and he swept me off the floor into his arms. Our family odyssey had ended. We knew very few families who hadn't lost someone, but our immediate family had been spared.

Oh, how good it was to have him home, back in his place as the head of our house. While Siegfried and I were no longer as dependent on our parents as we had been before the war, it felt good to have someone around who cared about us, who tried to protect us from the ugliness of life, and who, each night, with tears in his eyes, thanked God for his wife and his two boys.

On his first Sunday home, Father stayed behind while Mother and Siegfried and I walked into the school auditorium. Just as the worship service was about to begin, Father walked in.

The congregation went wild. They stepped over chairs, reached over people's heads, pushed each other gently to get to my father and greet him. It took about fifteen minutes to get the service started, and then it was a time of thanksgiving, celebration, and reunion all rolled into one.

Some things changed naturally with Father home. Siegfried and I moved out of his study and into our own room—the one with the hole in a wall. It was June, warm enough to live in a room without heat, and we got used to Mrs. Mueller's snoring on the other side of the closet.

The first relief shipments from America began to arrive, and my father quickly organized a committee to care for their distribution. He avoided doing it himself so that no one could say he took care of his own family first. In fact, he insisted that we receive none of these gifts. On those occasions when one of the ladies of the church gave me a handful of oats or sugar, I felt guilty as I slipped them into my mouth.

Before the cold came that fall, the church organized a cleanup operation on the old building. It would take a long time, but if everyone gave a little it could be done. Such cleanup campaigns were common in Berlin. To stem unemployment and clean up the rubble of war, the

165

government hired at a nominal wage anyone who was willing to work.

Our church program, however, was strictly a labor of love. We gathered afternoons with hammers, shovels, and picks, intent on freeing each unbroken brick and stacking it to be used for rebuilding. Often it meant climbing several stories on walls in danger of collapse.

On Saturdays at noon the women brought hot food to us, and my father came and worked with us. "It makes me a better preacher on Sundays if I work with you on Saturdays," he'd say. "But I'm going to let you younger men climb up on those walls. I'm too old for that."

The frost, then the snow, soon put a stop to the work, but we planned to resume in the spring.

In 1946 much of the daily life in Berlin revolved around trying to find food. One 28-year-old woman advertised in the newspaper for a "roommate," offering a two-room apartment and two CARE packages a month as part of the deal. The newspaper didn't publish her photo, but she nevertheless received 2,437 proposals of marriage!

My father's ration card classified him as a manual laborer, my mother's as an adult, and Siegfried's and mine as juveniles. The allocated portions on my ration card for one month contained the following items: bread, 25 pounds; fat, ¾ pound; meat, 1½ pounds; miscellaneous, 3½ pounds (usually flour, oats, etc.); cheese, 1½ pounds; sugar, 2 pounds; coffee substitute, ⅓ pound; potatoes, 20 pounds.

Item for item, adults received less than younger people. Hopefully they needed less, but as I watched my parents get thinner and thinner, I wasn't so sure about that.

Each month when we received our ration cards, we sat

166

down and carefully studied our allotments and any special instructions that came with them. Of course, the fact that a card allowed us to buy cheese, sugar, meat, and other items didn't necessarily mean the stores would have them. And often we stood in lines for many hours to discover that the item we had come for had long been sold out.

Still, God provided for our needs in marvelous ways. Friends supplied cauliflowers and turnips, and Siegfried and I picked edible weeds. We managed to get through the summer and fall without any sickness. We were often hungry, yes, but there was no threat of starvation.

We all agreed—God had truly prepared a table before us, as King David had said thousands of years before. Of course he also said, "My cup overflows." We didn't have that abundance, but for what we had, and for the fact that God himself was our shepherd, we gave thanks daily.

The winter of 1946–47 came early and hard, and the hardships suffered all over Europe are part of history. Siegfried and I moved back into Father's study with the understanding that if someone came seeking his pastoral help, we would immediately go to some other room.

Many came. We had women and teenage girls in our church who had been raped by Russian soldiers. Some had killed and others had stolen or lied, and they needed counseling. They all wanted to renew their relationship with Jesus Christ and deal with the horrors of the past and present.

Many more just gave up that winter. Suicides reached staggering rates. On January 6, one of the coldest days of the year, more than a thousand people in Berlin alone died of hunger and cold. The temperature dropped to 28 degrees below zero Fahrenheit on one occasion and the temperature inside Father's study was 27 degrees above. Schools closed. We went outdoors only for basic necessities, and we had electricity for only a few hours a day. I discovered that an empty stomach hates darkness even more than daylight. Somehow the hunger seemed to hurt more in the dark.

XX

More than two years had passed since I had watched my father walk away from the Villa Fragner. Our circle was complete, although at times I smiled, thinking, *We wanted to be together. But in one room?*

"How can you work with all of us milling around you?" I asked my father one day.

I expected one of those, "It's all right" answers, but instead he pulled me close to him and put his arm around me.

"Yes, Reini, it's hard to concentrate, but I get my real work done at night when I'm praying. That's when I receive clear guidance from God on what I should preach, and it's when I can help every church member most by bringing him before the throne of God."

That intimate moment of sharing moved me to tell my father about our Food Search Commandoes in

Austria and how I had experienced the real power of prayer. When I finished my story, he gripped my arm excitedly.

"Don't ever forget that experience, my son. Some day things will be better for us—they can't get much worse! But then people will forget the help they received from God. That's the way it was after World War I, and it will be the same again this time. Ingratitude is man's greatest sin."

As though by a prearranged signal, we both moved over to the sofa and knelt beside it. Many elbows had pressed into that worn upholstery in recent months, and tears stained its covers. Now we both thanked God again that he had kept our family alive and together.

I was aware that an important page of my life had turned and a new chapter had begun. I thought back and wondered what had happened to people such as Frau Bata, the talkative Czech cleaning woman, or to Kurt, our platoon leader. I had received a Christmas card from Captain Davis. He and his wife were doing fine without me.

At times I saw the faces of boys who hadn't come back—Tim, Horst, Rainer, Ronald. Some of the names I couldn't even remember. I had seen Juergen only once, and in a uniform at that. Hadn't we both pledged never to wear a uniform again?

Richard's leg had healed, and he was as strong as ever. Good old Richard the Lionhearted. He had dropped out of school, however, to take up a trade.

What a different route my friendship with Wolfgang had taken. From utter dislike and disgust, we had moved toward a very close friendship, hopefully for life.

When I looked back on my life up to that point, I was amazed at how much love and care God had put into the task of guiding and protecting me. Just before we left for Czechoslovakia, my father had given me a small card on which he had written a Bible verse. It was from a passage in Matthew in which Jesus says to his disciples, "Don't worry about tomorrow. God will take care of tomorrow. Live one day at a time."

"Soon we'll have to leave you," he told me. "To find the right balance in life, I've written down this rule for you."

I had stuck it in my Bible and often pulled it out to look at it. Once I had put it in my shirt pocket and forgotten about it when I turned the shirt in to be washed. When I remembered it, I hurried to the laundry room in the Villa Wagner and went through dozens of dirty shirts until I finally found it.

It was one of the items I had kept with me during all those months of wandering, and now I pulled it out to look at again. Was this the miracle of my survival, and perhaps the key to my healing in the bitter months after the fall of Germany?

One sore remained, however. From time to time I felt the hurt and the irritation and knew that I'd have to deal with it. With the pride of a young and dedicated Hitler Youth, I had despised the yellow Star of David. On many occasions I had joined the gang, mocking harmless Jews. But I had been an innocent child then who had known nothing of politics. Certainly I didn't know any better—or did I?

Shortly before Christmas 1947, a new student came to our class. I liked him the moment I saw him, and we were soon involved in friendly competition in language classes. He was a slightly built, darkhaired boy with a good sense of humor.

"How come you don't get a better mark in English?" he asked me one day. He already knew why and was teasing me. I had learned the American pronunciation,

171

which horrified my English teacher.

"But you're doing pretty well in German," he added.

"*You* do better in German," I countered.

He protested, so I shrugged and commented, "So we're both good in German. Why not? We're both Germans."

I noticed momentarily that he didn't answer, but I didn't give it much thought.

One Saturday I walked over to his house to give him a few books for a school assignment. He'd been sick and I had volunteered to help him make up lost time. A bearded old man with a small cap and long curls dangling down both sides of his head opened the door.

I must have stared at him for a moment, because he offered, "You must be Reinhold. Please come in. I'll take you to him."

As he shut the door to the bedroom, I burst out, "You didn't tell me you had a servant. What a strange man."

"He's my grandfather."

I wanted to crawl under the bed. "I'm sorry," I stammered. "It's just that he. . . ."

"Looks funny, right?" Paul helped me out.

"Right!"

Paul didn't say anything for a moment. Then he calmly told me, "He's an Orthodox Jew. Have you never seen one before?"

Instead of answering him, I asked, "And you are a Jew?"

"Yes, I am. My father was not Orthodox but my mother was."

"Where are your parents?" But even as I asked, I recalled that he had not mentioned them before and I had a sinking feeling.

"In Auschwitz."

"You mean. . . ."

"Yes."

I felt compelled to ask one more question, sensing again some hidden danger in it.

"Tell me, Paul, where is your grandfather from? His German sounds so different."

Paul smiled. "Did you ever hear of an A student in German who came from Czechoslovakia?"

Czechoslovakia! Rewnitz! The partisans! He was one of them, one of those, perhaps, who had stolen through the night to kill Hitler Youth such as myself.

Suddenly I knew what it was inside me that hurt. I had made friends with Russians, English, Americans, Austrians, with everyone but Czech Jews. I still could not bring myself to like Czech Jews.

"I had no idea," I said slowly.

"Would that have made a difference?" He looked at me carefully, and when I hesitated to answer, he got out of bed, crossed the room, and stood before me.

"Reinhold, you don't have to like me if you can't. I suppose I should have told you, but I still haven't forgiven the Nazis for killing my parents, and I don't like to talk about it. That's probably why I'm the all-German boy striving for the highest grade in German class. That may sound strange, but I thought it would help me forget."

My hand reached out and touched his. Who cared whether he was a Jew from Czechoslovakia? He was Paul, my friend. Dr. Gruenbaum had been my friend. So had little Esau in the second grade. They had drifted out of my life, but here was Paul. He needed a friend and he needed love to be healed of his mammoth hurts.

And I knew that in that love, the secret wound in me would be healed as well.

DENMARK

Stralsund

HAMBURG

NETHERLANDS

Wittenberg

Stendal

BERLIN

Braunschweig

Helmstedt

Magdeburg

WEST GERMANY

EAST GERMANY

Halle

Cologne

Dresden

Frankfurt

Nuremberg

FRANCE

Munich

Tyrlaching

Schladming

SWITZERLAND

St. Johann

SOVIET UNION

EAST
PRUSSIA

o Schwentainen

POLAND

o Warsaw

o Görlitz

o Prague
o Rewnitz

ZECHOSLOVAKIA

GERMANY

German boundaries of 1937

West Germany today

East Germany today

Poland today

Soviet Union today

Rewnitz (Czechoslovakia) is today known as
Revnice.

VIENNA

AUSTRIA

175

Epilogue

I believe everyone has at least one special project to
accomplish in his or her lifetime. In my case, it was
writing about the fifteen years when my life was being
shaped by two opposing worlds. When the one
world—the world marked by the swastika—broke
apart, the real conflict was over. The wounds left by
the years of the war began to heal.

Yet those wounds left scars. For as long as I live, I'll
remember the years I've written about. A word, a face,
a scene on film, or something from a book will remind
me of my struggle and the forces that tried to destroy
my soul. Sometimes the memories are oppressive, as
during my viewing of *Holocaust* or the more recent
Blood and Honor television movie.* Yet they also serve
as a reminder that God used my difficulties to
demonstrate his greatness in my life.

Many people who have read *Blood and Honor* ask the
question, "What happened to you in 1947 and the
following years?" In response, here is a brief account
of God's hand in the further course of my life.

THE AFTERMATH OF WAR

In 1948, my war-weary mind was ready for new
impressions. My friendship with the Czech-German
Jew, Paul, helped me to overcome my negative
feelings toward the race I had been programmed to
hate and the nation I resented most.

I also longed desperately to lead a more carefree
life. But looking for food and firewood after high
school kept me busy all year long, and left me little
time for games. The German survivors of World War

---

*The television movie is not related to my book, though both film and
book concern the Hitler youth.

II had added a word to the language: *Organisieren.* This rather official-sounding term covered a whole range of survival tactics, from canny manipulation of the ration system to the outright breaking of the law to secure food or other necessities.

Nonsmokers exchanged their cigarette rations for food or money. Collectors of stamps, china, and other valuables parted from them in exchange for potatoes or some butter or coffee. Wedding rings fell into the pockets of the black-market merchants in return for bread or meat. With the help of my father's unused ration of cigarettes, I, too, learned to "organize" to survive.

One day while I was carrying on this kind of business transaction, I got caught in an Allied military police raid. Hundreds of innocent pedestrians and not-so-innocent black marketeers were herded into trucks and taken to the M.P. station, where they had to give an account of their activities. There was really nothing illegal about my exchanging smoking goods for more nourishing items. Yet I felt the Allies might regard us as their enemies, and therefore guilty.

While a German policeman was interrogating me, a smiling American M.P. walked over and offered me a stick of chewing gum. I was surprised. Did he know that I was innocent? And what about the anti-fraternization law? Why did this American offer me a gift?

I slowly began to understand that there are good and bad people all over the world. I had seen Germans hate and kill Germans. But I had also seen starving, freezing Germans help each other in selfless love. I had met cold-hearted GIs who would not even look in my direction. But I had also met men like Frank, a U.S. Army sergeant and professional cook, who invited young people to his apartment every week for his culinary creations.

Frank was a Baptist, and attended the American-German youth church services in Berlin-Dahlem, which attracted many German teens—including me. I loved to sing the American hymns, which were so much more joyful than the German church hymns I was accustomed to. And I was intrigued by the down-to-earth and often humorous proclamation of the American chaplain.

Meanwhile, it did not take me long to realize that I was privileged to live in the American sector of Berlin. We were free to move about from one sector to the other, yet neither the Russian, British, nor French sectors felt as safe, relaxed, and friendly as the American.

The Russian government must have looked on our preferences with alarm. In June 1948, when the Western Allies introduced a new currency for their sectors of Berlin, the Russians prohibited the entry of food, water, fuel, power, and all other goods into the city through their zone, which surrounded all the others. They thought of this blockade as a sure way to get the entire city of Berlin under their control. But the Russians had not counted on General Lucius D. Clay's quick reaction. On the very same day, the American general arranged—in cooperation with the other Western Allies—the largest airlift in history.

Clay thought this "air bridge" would be needed for about three weeks. Instead, it lasted eleven months and demanded a daily cargo of 4,500 tons of supplies: food, paper, coal, gasoline, and more. Since my family lived close to the Berlin-Tempelhof Airport, our days and nights were filled with the humming of incoming and departing aircraft. American, British, and French planes made a total of 200,000 flights.

Along with the other West Berlin citizens, my family was willing to endure deprivation in order to stay on the side of the Western Allies: limited hours of electricity and heat, dried vegetables, powdered milk, drastic unemployment. I grew so used to the thundering sounds of low-flying planes that I woke at night only when fog or other problems hindered the planes from flying.

The American pilots—of whom seventy-six lost their lives—were more popular and celebrated in those months than film stars. People in the streets shook their hands or embraced and kissed them in emotional gratitude. One of the most popular was the "raisin bomber" pilot, Gale Halverson. Every day he dropped little parachutes made from handkerchiefs and loaded with candies or raisins. Soon his idea caught on with the other U.S. pilots. Children and teens waited for hours for such drops.

During the months of the airlift, my friendliness toward Americans turned into devotion. Many GIs sacrificed hours of their spare time to teach us youngsters how to throw a football or catch a baseball, which gave us a feeling of self-worth.

Finally, on May 11, 1949, the blockade was lifted. Soon the first army trucks reached Berlin with supplies. When these trucks headed back to West Germany, they carried big banners: "Hurrah, we're still alive!"

Living became fun again in 1949. I had my first girlfriend. I spent many free hours at radio RIAS (Radio in amerikanischen Sektor), where I belonged to the Music Youth Council, programming the music that was put on the air. At church I sang in the choir, taught Sunday school, and took on duties in the youth group.

In July 1950 I graduated from high school. There was no pomp. I celebrated at home with my family, eating the delicious cake Mother had baked for the occasion. Yet I was glad to have made it, in spite of many school transfers, air raids, and a nine-month period without school in 1945.

After graduation I made up my mind to continue my studies at a university. But I found out that because of my young age I had no chance of being admitted right away. Berlin was flooded with returned soldiers and also with refugees from East Germany, to whom the government offered preferred work and study opportunities. In January 1949 alone, 2,445 refugees from East Germany had sought asylum in Berlin.

Caught in this mass of applicants for school, I was pleased to be assured a place as a pharmaceutical apprentice within one year. To be independent and to help my parents financially, I took up various construction jobs in the meantime. The Berlin authorities had introduced *Notstandsprogramm* (Emergency Employment Program) to stem the flood of unemployment. People of all ages did various jobs and earned the same wage: 1.10 German marks. That was little enough, but I was glad to have found work.

People looked at the Notstandsprogramm workers as scum and openly showed their resentment. After all, most of my coworkers were ex-criminals, unable to find other jobs.

The working atmosphere was rough and dirty. Cursing, four-letter words, homosexuality, laziness, envy, and outright hatred were commonplace. I had thought that during the first fifteen years of my life I had seen the full depravity of man. Now I discovered that man could be just as evil in peacetime. I was especially amazed that the married men I worked with seemed to outdo each other in trying to influence us younger ones to accept their gutter life-style.

In the evenings, when I bicycled home, dead tired, I thanked the Lord that I wouldn't have to do that kind of work for the rest of my life. It was not just the labor that drained my strength, but the contact with people to whom nothing was sacred, people who seemed to glory in filth. Immediately after I reached home, I would take a shower to rinse off the construction dirt. Then I would dig into the Bible to wash off the inner dirt: the memories of filthy conversations and jokes that my mind had been forced to take in. I had not endured all the jeering and mocking at Hitler Youth camp to let my Christian convictions slip away now. Again God was using adversity to make me stronger in my devotion to him.

On July 1, 1951, I finally began my pharmaceutical apprenticeship. But another event that year was even more important in directing the course of my life. I received an invitation to the first European Baptist Youth Leaders Conference in Rueschlikon, Switzerland.

The conference was a heartwarming experience. Participants from twelve different countries shared and discussed leadership ideas. I could hardly believe that I, a German, was treated as a real brother and friend. I saw a blond girl from Holland, whose parents had suffered in German concentration camps, sing and pray in close fellowship with a muscular ex-paratrooper who had been a member of the German occupation army in Holland. And they loved each other—for Christ's sake!

The conference lasted for only one week. Yet, when I returned to Germany, I was more convinced than ever that "in Christ there is no East or West, in Him no South or North; but one great fellowship of love throughout the whole wide earth . . ."

As my apprenticeship in Berlin drew to a close, protests against the Russian restraint on German freedom grew. Finally, in June 1953, one thousand construction workers from East Berlin marched to the Labor Ministry and demanded higher wages, free elections, free access to associate with workers in West Berlin, and the right to strike. They triggered an avalanche of protest.

I was not brave enough or desperate enough to throw stones at the tanks, as many others did. But I quickly pedalled right into the heart of East Berlin to see history being made. In the evening of June 17, the border between East and West Berlin was brutally sealed with sharp-shooting policemen. Less than two hours before this ordinance I had made my way back to the American sector.

With tears of pity I learned the next day that the Russians had managed to quench the "monopol-capitalistic revolt of the workers" and had restored "peace and order."

Less than two weeks later I left Berlin to pursue further schooling in Frankfurt, where my father was now the pastor of a large Baptist church. It was a tremendous relief for me to be back in the free world, no longer on the small island of Berlin, squeezed in by hostile borders.

ON TO NEW LANDS

The response to my application at the Frankfurt University in 1953 was the same as it had been three years earlier in Berlin. Because of my young age and because of the many veteran and refugee applicants, I would have to wait still another year before being admitted to further pharmaceutical studies.

During the waiting period, I threw myself into the full-time work at the International Pharmacy in Frankfurt. And there was always plenty to do at the church. I became a preaching layman, serving one Sunday each month at one of the church's fourteen preaching stations in and around Frankfurt. The church's young people voted me their president. And I was also heavily involved in the preparation for Billy Graham's June 1954 crusade in Frankfurt.

These extracurricular activities continued when in the fall of 1954 I began courses at the university. And I added one more hobby that would prove beneficial to me later. Financing my own studies through part-time work in pharmacies, I set aside enough time and money for two trips per year across Europe and Africa as a tour guide.

In the course of my travels, I was stoned by a mob in Morocco, jailed in Spain (for picture taking), attacked by desert dogs in Egypt, robbed in Italy, serenaded in Spain, food-poisoned in France, proposed to in Norway, and made an honorary citizen of a town in Greece. In Sweden I met and later married Inger Birgitta Nilsson.

By 1958, the time of our wedding, I had completed my studies at Frankfurt and was working as a pharmacist in Wolfsburg, the city of Volkswagen fame. But the next year a major change took place: I gave up pharmaceutical work so that my wife and I could study theology in Rueschlikon, Switzerland. I had a tremendous desire to be part of the task force proclaiming God's plan of salvation to a spiritually starving world. Even though the switch from pharmacist to theology student and eventually pastor meant a drastic reduction of income, Inger and I were happy and satisfied in what we considered God's will.

It was during our studies at Rueschlikon that we were given the idea of emigrating to Canada to serve the bilingual Baptist churches there. On July 20, 1961, standing on board the *Olympia*, we waved good-bye to Swedish and German friends and relatives—and were off to find a new home in North America.

Everything on the North American continent was overpowering: the seemingly endless train ride from Montreal to Winnipeg in Manitoba; the first visit to a Canadian supermarket; the well-attended service at McDermot Avenue Baptist Church in Winnipeg, where, after a year at North American Baptist Seminary, I would serve as pastor; the openness and friendliness of the people.

McDermot Avenue Baptist Church, with four services each Sunday and a bilingual membership of over seven hundred, took up every minute of my next three years. I found little time to write even to the next-of-kin I had left behind in Germany. Father was in his last pastorate in Cologne, and my brother was serving a Baptist church in northern Germany.

Then God led us to another change. On a blustery cold January morning in 1965—31 degrees below zero—the moving van carrying our belongings plowed its way through the glistening dry snow, headed for Milwaukee, Wisconsin. There I served the German Zion Baptist Church.

During my pharmaceutical studies in Germany, I had worked as a free-lance writer for a newspaper and for various magazines. Now I picked up my hobby again, writing the monthly youth page for *Der Sendbote*, the German publication of the North

American Baptist Conference. Three years later I became its editor. Then I advanced from editor of German publications to director of all denominational publications, including the monthly *Baptist Herald*. My job took me all over North America and also abroad.

In October 1980, I joined the staff of the Baptist World Alliance (BWA) in Washington, D.C., as the associate secretary of communications, study, and research. The BWA serves as an umbrella organization for 124 Baptist groups in more than 141 countries. It was exciting for me to experience firsthand the life, work, needs, and joys of fellow believers in such places as the Dominican Republic, Haiti, Hungary, Romania, East Germany, and Poland.

It is also exciting to see how God has used my past to equip me for present and future ministry. Certainly my international background is helpful. I was born in Germany, so I'm German. But that part of Germany is now Polish, so the Poles claim me as their own. I have lived in Germany, Czechoslovakia, Switzerland, Canada, and the United States. My wife, Inger, is my Scandinavian connection. My three children were each born in a different land: Switzerland, the United States, and Canada.

In this past year, 1982, God used my German upbringing for another special part of his work.

HOMELANDS REVISITED

"Words alone cannot begin to express the profound feelings of sadness and revulsion that well up within me as I stand here at this monument of man's inhumanity to man." Those were Billy Graham's opening words as he and his team visited the former concentration camp at Sachsenhausen in the German Democratic Republic in October 1982.

As Graham's interpreter, I stood next to him. My feelings were just as stirred, but I could not afford to dwell on my emotions. My mind was racing ahead, anticipating his words, translating them into German and giving them a final polish in tone and inflection.

How had I come to be the interpreter for the "world famous Baptist evangelist," as the mass media in the German Democratic Republic called him?

Billy Graham was not a stranger to me. In 1954 I had worked many hours for his evangelistic rally in Frankfurt. In 1955 I had heard him at the Baptist World Congress in London. Five years later my wife and I had welcomed him to the small student body of the Baptist Theological Seminary in Rueschlikon. Press conferences in Tokyo, Stockholm, Urbana, and Moscow had given me more opportunities to observe the man who had won such world acclaim, and for years I had loved and admired him.

The Graham Association's choice of me as Graham's interpreter was, to me, God's hand in enlarging my ministry. From their point of view, I met certain crucial requirements: I was born and educated in Germany, had theological training, was at home in the German Bible, was accustomed to preaching in German, and knew the English language well.

But what about the German language? Was my German still good enough for this job? In spite of prayerful consideration, this question plagued me.

So I began to prepare myself for my task. For days I read nothing but German books and magazines. Next came the New Testament in German, a thick German dictionary, and Graham's books in the German language. I spent several days at the evangelist's office in Montreat, North Carolina, where I watched videotapes of his previous foreign language crusades.

While the Japanese interpreter spoke in Japanese, I would try to dub in my German interpretation of Graham's words.

Then the day of departure came. After a stopover in West Germany, I flew on to Vienna, where I met with Billy Graham for briefing sessions. I was impressed that he spent so much time in Bible study and prayer. In readying himself for his ministry in East Germany, he asked me one question after another about the situation there.

At the beginning of this preaching tour, Billy Graham told reporters that his purposes in coming were "to proclaim the gospel, to have fellowship with Christians, and to learn about the church situation." He did all this and more. There were luncheons, breakfasts, city tours, interviews, government receptions, church fellowship meetings, and press conferences—often leaving him on the brink of exhaustion. But each time he entered the pulpit to preach, God gave him miraculous strength.

Even though the German Democratic Republic is a relatively small country, we had to travel a lot: from Berlin to Halle, Wittenberg, Dresden, Gorlitz, Magdeburg, Stendal, Stralsund, and back to Berlin. Each sermon was delivered to overflow crowds, composed predominantly of youth.

"Aren't you surprised to see so many young people in our services?" Dr. Graham asked me one day. Yes, the high percentage of youth was even more astonishing to me than the hundreds and thousands of people who now crowded into churches that at other times were scarcely filled. Almost four decades of atheistic teaching in schools and youth movements had not quelled the young people's interest in God.

With deep emotion, I thought back on my own

youth. Even then God had proved to be stronger than atheistic teachings and slogans.

I enjoyed interpreting for Billy Graham because I discovered at close range that he is a totally honest man. Whether he was kneeling at the memorial in Sachsenhausen, speaking to pastors and deacons at a luncheon, or proclaiming the good news in East Germany's largest Lutheran churches, he always meant what he said and did.

Precious were the moments when we held hands in prayer or when we knew that silence would be more refreshing than talk during a lengthy car trip. He would stretch out his long legs as far as possible, roll up a coat or whatever else was available as a pillow, and try to sleep. At such times I, too, would relax or take time to pray for his ministry and my own.

During these long rides, Graham probed frequently into my past. He had read the original edition of *Blood and Honor* twice, and seemed genuinely interested in every facet of my life. I was amazed. He had so many things to think of, yet he took time to know the people with whom he worked.

When evangelist Billy Graham waved good-bye to me at the Berlin-Schonefeld airport after the ten-day East German crusade, he was ready to carry his preaching ministry into Czechoslovakia. I had declined his invitation to accompany him. On the following day I was to fly to Poland for a one-week visit with fellow believers there.

Our ways parted. But our tasks were complementary: his as an evangelist to call people back to God, mine as a Baptist World Alliance official to look after the physical and spiritual well-being of fellow Christians in a country marked by need.

Germany, Czechoslovakia, Poland. In some ways all

three nations were "home" to me—and had been the sites for great campaigns to undermine the gospel. Yet as I watched Dr. Graham board that plane, I had high hopes for his mission: hope in the staying power of God's love and truth.

I remembered my own visit to Czechoslovakia six months earlier, my first time back there since the end of the war. All my duties as an official of the Baptist World Alliance had been set aside the day we were taken on a tour to Rewnitz (now Revnice).

As I had walked the familiar streets of Revnice, I had relived both the excitement of my boyhood and its sad ending. The railroad station had not changed a bit. I could still imagine us Hitler Youth running around in 1945, hoping for reasonable space in the overcrowded train cars. It felt strange to walk on the sidewalks now rather than march stiffly down the middle of the streets.

That day we had stopped at a Catholic church, which had been off-limits to me as a Hitler Youth in 1944-45. In all those months in Czechoslovakia I had never been permitted to attend church. "A German boy doesn't need that pious stuff," I had been told.

A little later our tour party had eaten—just as I had many years ago—at the Volkshaus, which is now a hotel. During our meal we had begun a cautious conversation with three elderly gentlemen at the next table. While two of them hesitated to talk, the face of the third had softened as he seemed to remember earlier years.

After another stroll, we had arrived at Villa Fragner. The familiar iron gate faced me, and the same house; only the large garden had changed, now subdivided into many plots. We were welcomed warmly by the present owner.

The second floor stood empty, almost the way we had left it thirty-seven years before. I stood on the spot where my bed had been, opened the window, and enjoyed the unchanged panoramic view of the surrounding hills.

Suddenly the familiar sound of a radio announcement, warning of approaching bombers, had flashed into my mind, and I had surprised my hosts by repeating the alert in almost flawless Czech. Ghosts of the past! But there were no attacking planes now. Instead we had sipped coffee and chatted.

When we had left Revnice behind us, I had felt a strange sense of exhilaration. The visit had taught me again that people choose their own courses of development, in spite of their circumstances. Two of the men in the restaurant had hesitated to talk to us. Had they not been able to forgive the Germans for occupying their city and thus making it a target of Allied bombings? The third man had conversed freely. Why?

I had not known the answer to those questions. But I did know what had helped me choose my response to the war. Many years ago a couple had pledged to "train up a child in the way he should go." My parents had instilled in me the Word of God and set an example of Christian living before my eyes.

As I waved to Dr. Graham at the airport, I realized that this is our mutual hope for the future. We believe that God's truth, once sown, will survive and thrive through the power of the Holy Spirit.

January 1983
Reston, Virginia

Above Left: The inscription on this photo, taken on my second birthday, reads "The Young Germany." *Right:* Siegfried, 11, poses in his Hitler Youth uniform in 1939.

Left: Freshly drafted into the Hitler Youth in 1942, my face shows the seriousness of the new Germany. *Right:* Our apartment in Berlin-Neukolln overlooked these trees in 1944—before they were felled by bombs and fuel scavengers.

Above: The Villa Fragner in Rewnitz once housed 100 boys. Now only one elderly widow lives there, but she welcomed us on our return trip in 1982.

Left: Father stands proudly with his two sons on the day before he took me to Czechoslovakia in August 1944. *Right:* Shortly after Father's return from Italy in 1946, our reunited family poses in front of the ruins of our church.